Organic Apple Production Manual

TECHNICAL COORDINATORS AND AUTHORS

SEAN L. SWEZEY, Specialist, Center for Agroecology & Sustainable Food Systems, University of California, Santa Cruz; Director, University of California Sustainable Agriculture and Education Program, Davis

PAUL VOSSEN, University of California Cooperative Extension Farm Advisor, Sonoma County

JANET CAPRILE, University of California Cooperative Extension Farm Advisor, Contra Costa County

WALT BENTLEY, University of California Cooperative Extension Area IPM Specialist, Kearney Ag Center, Parlier

PREPARED AT THE CENTER FOR AGROECOLOGY & SUSTAINABLE FOOD SYSTEMS
UNIVERSITY OF CALIFORNIA, SANTA CRUZ

UNIVERSITY OF CALIFORNIA
AGRICULTURE AND NATURAL RESOURCES
PUBLICATION 3403

For information about ordering this publication, contact

University of California
Agriculture and Natural Resources
Communication Services—Publications
6701 San Pablo Avenue, 2nd Floor
Oakland, California 94608-1239

Telephone: 800-994-8849 or 510-642-2431
FAX: 510-643-5470
E-mail: danrcs@ucdavis.edu
Visit the ANR Communication Services website at http://anrcatalog.ucdavis.edu

Publication 3403

ISBN 1-879906-48-1
Library of Congress Catalog Card No. 99-076533

WARNING ON THE USE OF CHEMICALS

Pesticides are poisonous. Always read and carefully follow all precautions and safety recommendations given on the container label. Store all chemicals in their original labeled containers in a locked cabinet or shed, away from foods or feeds, and out of the reach of children, unauthorized persons, pets, and livestock.

Recommendations are based on the best information currently available, and treatments based on them should not leave residues exceeding the tolerance established for any particular chemical. Confine chemicals to the area being treated. THE GROWER IS LEGALLY RESPONSIBLE for residues on the grower's crops as well as for problems caused by drift from the grower's property to other properties or crops.

Consult your county agricultural commissioner for correct methods of disposing of leftover spray materials and empty containers. Never burn pesticide containers.

PHYTOTOXICITY: Certain chemicals may cause plant injury if used at the wrong stage of plant development or when temperatures are too high. Injury may also result from excessive amounts or the wrong formulation or from mixing incompatible materials. Inert ingredients, such as wetters, spreaders, emulsifiers, diluents, and solvents, can cause plant injury. Since formulations are often changed by manufacturers, it is possible that plant injury may occur even though no injury was noted in previous seasons.

3m-pr-3/00-GM/KT

CONTENTS

PREFACE

Beginning in the 1992 apple production season, the U.S. Department of Agriculture's Sustainable Agriculture Research and Education (USDA-SARE) Western Region Research Grants Program, with the collaborative support of the U.S. Environmental Protection Agency's Agriculture in Concert with Environment Program, granted support for a three-year investigation and extension project titled "Farm-Level Function and Performance of Certified Organic Apple Production in California." This research grant was made to an interdisciplinary team of four University of California specialists and farm advisors (Sean L. Swezey, Paul Vossen, Janet Caprile, and Walt Bentley) with research and extension duties in California apples in each major apple production region (Central Coast, North Coast, Northern San Joaquin Valley, and Southern San Joaquin Valley, respectively). We would like to thank Dave Schlegel and Phil Rasmussen, Western SARE administrators, for their support of this project.

This manual is in part the product of observations, direct fieldwork, and in-progress or published research results of this unique working group. Contributing authors helped round out the publication with information based on their own research programs.

HOW TO USE THIS MANUAL

This manual is intended to be used by current or potential producers of certified organic apples. Many of the basic agronomic practices are the same for both organic and conventional apple production systems; these are well outlined in *Commercial Apple Growing in California* (ANR Publication 2456, 1992). This manual, which emphasizes organic production practices, is designed to be used as a companion to *Commercial Apple Growing in California* and *Integrated Pest Management for Apples and Pears,* 2nd ed. (ANR Publication 3340, 1999). Other publications that the organic grower may find of interest are listed in the bibliography. Together with this manual, these publications provide a good reference kit for anyone considering the practical methods and implications of organic apple production.

Where techniques for organic production differ critically from conventional practices (especially regarding replacement of synthetic materials with organically acceptable materials for soil fertility, pest control, and postharvest handling), this manual emphasizes methods that are available and effective in commercial organic contexts under present regulations in California. Major chapter headings and content are devoted to these alternative production approaches.

The suggestions in this manual have been formulated over the past 20 years and are a culmination of work by many researchers. Grants from private foundations, state and federal sustainable agriculture programs, and the University of California's Sustainable Agriculture Research and Education Program (UC SAREP), funded the research on which this manual is based.

CONSIDERATIONS IN ORGANIC APPLE PRODUCTION

Modern commercial apple production is a technical undertaking. Growers must use knowledge about the compatibility of varieties and specific soil types in specific climates, of how tree spacing is influenced by soil and rootstock, of variety growth characteristics, of pollinators that bloom at the same time as main varieties, and of training and pruning to limit tree size and maximize light in the lower tree canopy. Knowledge and practice of organically acceptable insect and disease controls are also essential. In addition, growers must manage labor economically and market organic fruit effectively. A foundation of good horticultural practices based on an understanding of apple nutrition, soils, cover crops, water management, and insect and disease life cycles is needed to develop successful practices that create a healthy orchard ecosystem.

California organic apple production is highly regional in nature due to differing costs of production (especially in land values and orchard size) and climate-related pest incidence and pressures. Additional differences exist in economies of scale and market niches available for particular varieties, sizes, or grades.

Because of the technical and local nature of organic production, the authors recommend that growers planning to convert to organic methods use the information presented in this manual while simultaneously acquiring actual production experience in a carefully planned transitional or conversion period in a selected orchard (a minimum of 3 years under state regulations). Where possible, growers entering the organic market for the first time should seek advice from established growers or observe established organic production orchards in the local area.

Many organic production techniques are not fertility or pest-crisis oriented in the short term; organic apple growers often seek more long-term adjustment of soil quality or pest levels using techniques that are slow to act, not apparent in initial effect, or locally novel. For this reason, a site-specific conversion study to compare similarly sized blocks of orchard under conventional and organic management practices should be the starting point for any transition plan.

Care should be taken to minimize economic risks involved in conversion until enough season-to-season experience has been gained. Initial caution is recommended with respect to oversizing of converted blocks (we recommend blocks of 10 to 20 acres to start), expanding only if economic results are favorable.

Experienced organic apple growers with certified acreage in production will recognize this manual as a descriptive inventory of the methods legally available for organic apple production in California. However, there are a number of other reasons that apple growers may want to consider these methods even if organic certification is not the goal. Apple growers can apply these methods where concerns about pest resistance to pesticides, secondary pest creation and outbreak, postharvest residues, farmer, farmworker, or rural resident health and safety, or other regulatory restrictions may motivate production systems changes.

"Organically grown" is a legal status currently regulated by the state; a decision to pursue organic registration and certification should consider all relevant state and federal regulations, materials lists, certifiers, markets and marketers, and economic conditions, including present and predicted supply and demand. It is the expressed intent of this manual to assist California apple growers in the consideration and application of techniques acceptable for organic certification; actual production and marketing decisions remain with the individual grower or manager. This manual can serve as a primary information source in the context of larger decisions about the future character of apple production in California.

AUTHORS

TECHNICAL COORDINATORS AND AUTHORS

SEAN L. SWEZEY, Specialist, Center for Agroecology & Sustainable Food Systems, University of California, Santa Cruz; Director, University of California Sustainable Agriculture and Education Program, Davis

PAUL VOSSEN, University of California Cooperative Extension Farm Advisor, Sonoma County

JANET CAPRILE, University of California Cooperative Extension Farm Advisor, Contra Costa County

WALT BENTLEY, University of California Cooperative Extension Area IPM Specialist, Kearney Ag Center, Parlier

CONTRIBUTING AUTHORS

CHUCK INGELS, University of California Cooperative Extension Farm Advisor, Sacramento County

DESMOND JOLLY, Director, University of California Cooperative Extension, Small Farm Center, Davis

KAREN KLONSKY, Cooperative Extension Specialist, Department of Agricultural and Resource Economics, University of California, Davis

WARREN MICKE, Extension Pomologist, Department of Pomology, University of California, Davis

ELIZABETH MITCHAM, Associate Specialist and Pomolgist, University of California, Davis

LAURA TORTE, Small Farms Advisor, University of California Cooperative Extension, Santa Cruz County

RON TYLER, University of California Cooperative Extension (Emeritus)

LUCIA VARELA, IPM Advisor, University of California Cooperative Extension and Statewide IPM Project, Sonoma County

KATHLEEN WALKER, University of California, Berkeley

DESLEY WHISSON, Vertebrate Pest Specialist, Department of Wildlife, Fish, and Conservation Biology, University of California, Davis

EDITED AND PREPARED BY

SEAN L. SWEZEY, Specialist

MARTHA BROWN, Senior Editor

Center for Agroecology & Sustainable Food Systems

University of California, Santa Cruz

ACKNOWLEDGMENTS

Many growers and investigators contributed to the research-based guidelines in this manual. We would like to thank the following apple growers for their cooperation and efforts.

Tony Banovac, Charles Bertoli, Jim Carlisle, Don Chandler, Bill Denevan, John Diffenbaugh, Jim Erybide, Bob Gilardoni, Nick Gilardoni, Mitch Gizdich, Vince Gizdich, Greg House, George Jewell, Perry Kozlowski, Jim Nelson, Dago Oseguera, Dick Rider, Jim Rider, Anselmo Rivas, Lewis Scherrill, Ed Silva, and John Wood.

We would also like to express our appreciation to the following research colleagues who generously gave their time to specific research and implementation questions addressed in the manual: Sue Blodgett, Marc Buchanan, Kate Burroughs, Janice Gillespie, Joe Grant, Jay Irvine, Sandra McDougall, Nicholas Mills, Don Thompson, and Matthew Werner.

The Clarence E. Heller Charitable Foundation and the Organic Farming Research Foundation supported additional research activities on which guidelines in this manual are based. We thank Bruce Hirsch and Bob Scowcroft for their support.

....

CREDITS

Jack Kelly Clark: color plates 2.1, 2.2, 2.3, 2.4, 2.5, 3.2, 3.5, 3.6; black and white photos on pp. 2, 8, 38, 46, 54.

Elizabeth Mitcham: color plates 4.1, 4.2, 4.3.

Sean Swezey: color plates 2.6, 2.9, 2.10, 3.7, 3.8.

Paul Vossen: color plates 2.7, 2.8, 2.11, 3.1, 3.3, 3.4.

1

Overview of the Organic Apple Industry

By the year 2000, California will likely emerge as the nation's second-largest apple producing state after Washington, with 10 to 12 percent of U.S. production for a total exceeding 500,000 tons. Bearing acreage has increased by over 50 percent since 1986 due to new Granny Smith and Fuji plantings in the San Joaquin Valley. Apple production is currently widespread in the state, with 35,700 bearing acres in 1998 and gross values ranging from $138 to $170 million per year from 1992 to 1996. The three largest production regions are the San Joaquin Valley, the Central Coast, and the North Coast.

In 1998, the California Organic Program (COP) of the California Department of Food and Agriculture listed over 4,000 registered acres of organic apples in the state. The total value of organic apple products grown, processed, handled, or distributed in California was nearly $15 million in 1998 (source: Ray Green, COP, pers. comm.).

Annual per capita consumption of fresh apples in the United States increased by 18 percent from the early 1970s to the late 1980s, when it leveled out at about 20 pounds per person, where it remains today. During that same period, the consumption of processed apple products almost doubled due largely to an increase in sales of apple juice.

TRENDS IN ORGANIC PRODUCTION AND MARKETS

Making up a small but growing percentage of statewide acreage, certified organic apple production represents an emerging technical and marketing alternative for California apples. The 1989 controversy surrounding detectable residues of daminozide (Alar) metabolites in apple products stimulated market interest in certified organic apples for both fresh-market and processing fruit.

Following the Alar crisis, demand for fresh and processed organic apples increased, as did prices. Many mainstream supermarkets introduced organically grown apples into their produce sections. Some found that consistency of quality, supply, and price premiums did not fit smoothly into their produce programs and stopped carrying organically produced fresh apples. But while organic apples are not as readily available in supermarket chain stores today, other outlets such as consumer cooperatives, natural food stores, specialty produce stores, and direct markets continue to make organic apple products available to consumers.

Organically produced apple products can still be regarded as mainly occupying niche markets—geographic, demographic, and other consumer niches. Prior to 1990, environmentally concerned consumers were the primary market. Since then, middle- and upper-middle-income households, particularly those with young children, have joined the ranks of those purchasing organic apple products. Children face a higher possible health risk from accumulated dietary chemical residues in fresh and processed foods. Not surprisingly, foods consumed at higher rates by children have been targeted for changes in marketing and production practices. Hence, organic fresh apples, applesauce, and apple juice have all experienced substantial increases in demand.

The growing popularity of organic apple products mirrors explosive growth in the organic foods market. According to the Organic Farming Research Foundation, organic foods sales increased from $178 million in 1980 to $1 billion in 1990, and quadrupled between 1990 and 1997 to $4 billion. Of that amount, organic produce accounts for approximately $680 million annually. Organic products now average around 5 percent of all new food and beverage product introductions.

SUPPLY AND PRICE RESPONSE

Most of the more than 600 organic fruit growers in California are small-scale producers. Seventy-six percent have sales of less than $25,000 per year on an average-sized farm of 25 acres or less. Larger growers are also becoming certified organic producers, which could lead to competition for existing markets and lower prices for organic fruit.

California's organic apple production has grown rapidly since 1990, keeping pace with increased conventional production. The national organic product economy has grown more than 20 percent per year in that same period of time.

REGULATION OF CALIFORNIA ORGANIC APPLES

Commodities produced and marketed as organic are currently regulated by two laws: the California Organic Foods Act (COFA) of 1990 and the federal Organic Foods Production Act (OFPA) of 1990. The date for implementation and enforcement of the federal law is still uncertain and will depend on the finalizing and adoption of National Organic Standards by the U.S. Department of Agriculture (USDA).

The laws establish production standards for any product marketed or sold as organic and give legal label definitions to the terms "organic farming" and "organic foods." This protects producers, handlers, processors, and sellers against fraud while assuring consumers that organic products meet specific criteria. In addition, the laws make it easier for organic foods to be transported and sold throughout the United States.

At both the state and federal levels, advisory boards have compiled lists of approved and prohibited materials for use in organic agriculture. Growers who choose

to produce and market their crops as organic must register with the state. Federal law will require certification.

State Registration

Growers who produce and market organic commodities are required to register each year with the California Department of Food and Agriculture and must adhere to specific organic production procedures and standards outlined in the California Organic Foods Act of 1990. Penalties may result for those in violation of the law. A copy of the law and a list of approved and prohibited materials may be obtained from the California Department of Food and Agriculture's Organic Program (CDFAOP). Ask for the publication *California Organic Program: Producing, Handling, and Processing Organic Products in California*, CDFAOP 1996.

The state program is grower-funded by annual registration fees and is administered by the California Department of Food and Agriculture's Organic Program. Initial registration takes place at the local level through the county agricultural commissioner. Registration data are then centralized in Sacramento, where subsequent registrations are handled. Annual farm or business inspections are not mandatory under the COFA; however, the California Organic Program recently enacted a policy whereby unannounced inspections may be performed at any time. Enforcement is based on confirmed violations of the law.

Annual state registration fees are based on a graduated scale of a grower's gross sales during the previous year. Fees range from $25 for sales of $10,000 or less to $2,000 for sales over $5 million. First-year registrants must pay a one-time-only assessment of one and one-half times the amount indicated on the graduated scale. If no sales occurred in the previous year, fee remittance is based on the projected gross receipts.

Federal Regulation

The federal OFPA became effective on October 1, 1993. However, implementation and enforcement have been delayed by the rule-making process. When implemented, the OFPA could preempt California state law except in those cases where the state applies to the USDA for approval of stricter standards. It would be prudent for growers to comply with both federal and state regulations at this time.

The OFPA is administered by the USDA's National Organic Program. At present, no federal registration is required for organic growers nor are any assessment fees charged. However, to be in compliance with the OFPA in its current form, all producers with annual gross sales of more than $5,000 would have to be certified by an accredited certifying agent. Depending on the certification agency, stipulations often include, but are not limited to, participation in annual farm inspections, periodic pesticide residue testing, and assessment of reasonable fees. Federal or any other certification is separate from and should not be confused with state registration. Additionally, some exceptions to the 3-year transition period (see **Organic Certification** below) exist in the federal law, and growers should consult federal, state, and independent certification agencies about allowable exceptions.

Organic Certification

There are a number of certification organizations registered with the state of California. None are currently accredited by the USDA because the USDA's certification program has not yet been implemented. At present, each organization must adhere to all state and federal laws regulating organic commodities and in addition may enforce standards and procedures specific to their own agencies. Additional fees are charged by the certification agency for their own marketing and for inspection of the farm and farm records. Although certification is not required by California state law, most growers choose to be certified in order to meet marketplace standards.

The certification process begins upon submission of an application package to a certification agency. The application package is reviewed and accepted by a certification committee, board, panel, or individual. Actual organic certification is awarded only after all state, federal, and certifying agency standards have been met and a 3-year transition period is completed. It is the sole responsibility of the grower to comply with applicable production standards and to provide the appropriate data to satisfy organic certification requirements. Growers are expected to keep accurate records of all inputs into the land and trees.

Growers committed to organic apple production should begin the certification process as soon as possible due to the lengthy minimum time period for transitioning from conventional to organic farming methods. During the transition period fruit can be labeled "transitional," but this usually carries no price premium.

The following guidelines may be useful for apple growers considering organic production and certification.

1. Obtain and study state and federal laws, materials lists, and the standards and procedures for one or more certification agencies; choose the certification agency that best suits your individual farming operation and marketing plan.

2. Follow all rules and regulations pertinent to state and federal laws as well as those of the selected certification agency.

3. Compile a crop history for each field, production, or management unit.

4. Keep detailed records of production practices and inputs. For example, document all material applications in terms of the product name, the application date, location, purpose, and per acre rate. Appropriate documentation for the farming operation is essential for organic certification.

5. Be prepared for farm inspections. Inspections include requests for documentation of material inputs and production practices and may include soil testing. Note that farm inspectors do not actually certify growers; their primary function is to document compliance with the law and report these findings to the certifying agent for review.

6. Register as an organic producer with the state of California as soon as you begin marketing products as organic.

2

Orchard Management

Organic and conventional apple production systems share many aspects. The basic considerations of orchard culture, including orchard establishment, variety and rootstock selection, pruning, tree nutrition, irrigation, orchard floor management, crop regulation, and replanting, are well addressed in *Commercial Apple Growing in California* (ANR Publication 2456). The information presented here includes those additional considerations unique or particularly relevant to organic production.

ORCHARD CULTURE

Site Selection

The multiple climatic zones and microclimates within California can significantly affect fruit quality and pest pressures that, in turn, can greatly affect the profit potential of an organic apple orchard. Controlling codling moth and apple scab, two of the most prevalent pest and disease problems, is much easier in cool, dry climates. Here are some of the factors to consider when selecting a site:

- Land that has deep, well-drained soil with naturally high fertility, high organic matter content, and excellent water quality and availability offers an advantage to all growers, but especially to the organic grower.

- Codling moth has more generations (up to four) in the warmest areas of California, such as the Central Valley and Southern California. The cooler coastal areas have only two or sometimes three generations of moths and their larvae (worms). Where codling moth pressures are very high, control of the first generation is extremely important. In low-pressure areas, the first generation is sometimes ignored.

- Isolating large blocks of trees from other orchards and their pests is a very positive step since this will reduce or eliminate movement of moths or fungus spore inoculum into the new orchard. Orchards have an advantage if they are located at least ½ mile (0.8 km) from other apple, pear, or walnut orchards or backyard fruit trees.

- The pheromone-based mating disruption technique works much better on large solid blocks (greater than 10 acres [4 ha]) of trees because the edge effect is reduced.

- Flat land offers an advantage for pheromone-based mating disruption since the pheromone is heavier than air and in uneven terrain dissipates or flows downhill with the contour of the land.

- Orchards located in areas with less spring rainfall will avoid attack by the apple scab fungus. Mild weather during bloom aids fruit set, reduces fire blight disease, and moderates alternate bearing.

- The ability to grow a winter cover crop to provide lower-cost nutrition and soil enhancement compared to applying organic fertilizers or compost is also important. Cold winter locations with snow or very hard freezes can limit winter cover crop usage.

- When possible, avoid sites infested with problem weeds such as bermudagrass (*Cynodon dactylon*), field bindweed (*Convolvulus arvensis*), or Johnsongrass (*Sorghum halepense*), as well as nematodes, *Armillaria* (oak root fungus), and *Dematophora*, as these persistent problems are usually not adequately controlled by any available organic methods.

Land Preparation

Many potential problems can be reduced or eliminated by careful preparation of the orchard site prior to planting. The preparation period is a good time to improve drainage, incorporate organic matter, add nutrients, adjust soil acidity or alkalinity, and control weeds. Remove as many roots as possible from old orchard sites or wooded areas to limit holdover material for oak root fungus.

If possible, begin to prepare at least 1 to 2 years in advance of planting trees. You may want to plant a tall-growing cover crop such as bell beans in the winter months to increase the organic matter content in the soil. If water is available, grow a summer cover crop such as Sudangrass to smother and weaken perennial weeds. Try to order nursery trees 2 years in advance to get the best selection of varieties and to be able to plant trees with some side branches.

Soil solarization can benefit the growth of newly planted trees by reducing the incidence of most annual and some perennial weeds, nematodes, and harmful soil disease organisms such as *Phytophthora* root rot. Solarization involves tarping tilled and irrigated land with clear plastic for a month or more in midsummer. A detailed description of soil solarization requirements, timing, and methods can be found in *Soil Solarization: A Nonpesticidal Method for Controlling Diseases, Nematodes, and Weeds* (ANR Publication 21377, 1997).

At a minimum, the soil should be tested for mineral content (phosphorous, potassium, calcium, and magnesium) and pH. Micronutrient levels should also be determined if a problem is suspected. Other tests for both soil and water include tests for EC (electrical conductivity, a measure of salt content), SAR (sodium absorption ratio), bicarbonate levels, sodium and chloride levels, and boron. These tests are done to avoid excess or deficiency situations and to provide a basis for corrective action prior to planting.

A much more accurate measure of plant nutritional status is to test the tissue of apple tree leaves in an existing planting. For corrective procedures, sampling methodologies, and desired values for nutrients in soil and water, see *Soil and Plant Tissue Testing in California* (ANR Publication 1879, 1983) and *Water Quality: Its Effects on Ornamental Plants* (ANR Publication 2995, 1985).

Large quantities of manure or compost (up to 20 tons/acre [44,800 kg/ha]) are very beneficial to the growth response in young trees and should be incorporated into the soil before planting. These amendments provide a slow release of nitrogen and some of the phosphorous and potassium necessary for the first year or two of growth. Organic amendments should be incorporated into the soil by disking or other tillage equipment in order to prevent the nitrogen from volatilizing into the air.

Soils low in phosphorous or potassium should be corrected with heavy applications of these minerals from organically certifiable sources. Phosphorous commonly comes from soft rock phosphate and potassium from mined potassium sulfate (see **Tree Nutrition and Fertilization** later in this chapter).

Soil pH should be adjusted to between 5.5 and 7.5 through the addition of lime to raise pH or soil sulfur to lower it. Lime requirements can be calculated by a diagnostic laboratory from soil samples, and application rates depend on soil type and the original pH value. Organic matter typically associated with raising or lowering pH works very slowly (over a period of hundreds of years), which makes their use for that purpose unreasonable.

Apple trees will grow and produce well in a wide range of calcium- and magnesium-containing soils. Calcium and magnesium levels are sometimes adjusted to a 5 to 1 ratio in favor of calcium, but this can be expensive and comparable benefits are not always evident (see the discussion of bitter pit under **Major Physiological Disorders** in chapter 3 for calcium recommendations).

Planting

Trees should be planted when dormant. Composts or amended soils should not be placed in the planting hole because they create such a good environment for root growth that the roots stay within the planting hole and grow in a circle. If available, apply 3 to 4 inches (7.5 to 10 cm) of compost or mulch to the soil surface just after planting.

Immediately after planting, paint the trunks of dormant trees with water-based interior paint or commercial whitewash from the soil line to the top of the trunk to protect them from sunburn and attack by wood boring insects.

Good irrigation, fertilization, and weed control are vital for vigorous tree growth during the first year. Weeds compete with young trees for soil moisture and nutrients and should be eliminated within 2 to 3 feet (0.6 to 0.9 m) of the trunk by mulching, burning, or cultivation, especially for the first 3 years of growth. Allowing weeds to compete with young trees can reduce tree growth by as much as 50 percent.

Rootstock Selection

Dwarfing or semidwarfing rootstocks are now commonly used for most new or replacement plantings of apples. These stocks produce smaller trees than standard, or seedling, rootstocks. They also come into bearing earlier to provide a quicker return on investment.

The smaller trees can improve fruit color, enhance pest and disease control through better spray coverage, and eliminate or reduce the size of ladders for increased orchard safety, efficiency, and convenience. All the size-controlling rootstocks require regular irrigation and are not suitable for dry-farmed sites. For greater detail regarding the horticultural characteristics of apple rootstocks, refer to *Commercial Apple Growing in California* (ANR Publication 2456, 1992).

Choosing the proper rootstock may allow the apple grower to avoid potential pest or disease problems. Resistance to woolly apple aphid, Phytophthora root rot, and fire blight are perhaps the most important rootstock characteristics to select for because there are no suitable organic controls for these pests. The common rootstocks available in California and their important pest avoidance characteristics are described below.

Seedling (Standard) Rootstock. This was the only stock used for many years in California apple orchards. It produces large, very vigorous, full-sized trees that do not come into bearing until the trees are 7 to 10 years old. Today, standard rootstock is used only in nonirrigated or low vigor sites or for spur-type varieties. Its one advantage is a greater tolerance for wet feet and Phytophthora root rot compared to dwarfing stocks. It is very susceptible to woolly apple aphid and moderately susceptible to fire blight.

M111. M111 is a semidwarfing rootstock that usually produces a tree 80 percent the size of a tree on seedling. It tolerates varying soil conditions and resists woolly apple aphid. It was typically planted in the Central Valley because it is more resistant to the *Phytophthora* root rot species found there, but its excess vigor is a problem. It is also somewhat resistant to fire blight.

M106. M106 is a semidwarfing rootstock that produces a tree about 65 to 75 percent the size of a tree on seedling, but without proper care it will not reach its size potential. This rootstock is resistant to woolly apple aphid and somewhat resistant to fire blight, but has been susceptible to root rot caused by some *Phytophthora* species. It has been less susceptible to root rot in the coastal growing areas, presumably due to the presence of different *Phytophthora* species.

M7a. M7a is a semidwarfing rootstock that produces a tree about 60 percent the size of a seedling rooted tree. It performs well in irrigated replant situations but tends to sucker. It is resistant to fire blight but susceptible to woolly apple aphid.

M26. M26 is a semidwarfing to dwarfing rootstock that produces a tree 30 to 50 percent the size of a tree on seedling. It has performed very poorly in most situations in California and is extremely susceptible to fire blight.

M9. M9 is a dwarfing rootstock that produces a very small tree less than 30 percent the size of a seedling-rooted tree. It is poorly anchored with a brittle root system and must be trellised. It stunts if not adequately managed but has become the most common commercially planted rootstock in the world because of its excellent performance, efficiency, and precocity.

Mark. Mark is a rootstock similar in size to M9, but it has been a very poor performer in California and other apple growing regions in the world.

Virus-free forms of most of the semidwarfing and dwarfing rootstocks are available and are indicated by the letters EMLA in front of the rootstock number. These virus-free rootstocks tend to be longer lived and 10 to 15 percent more vigorous than the original, virus-infected releases of the same clones (preceded by M or MM). However, if the variety grafted onto the rootstock is not virus free, it will infect the rootstock, and the expected benefits will be lost. Use only certified, virus-free grafting wood with EMLA rootstocks.

Variety Selection

Choosing the right variety is one of the most important decisions for the organic apple producer. The variety should be adapted to the climate of the district where it will be grown, and it should enjoy good market demand. Apples grown in cooler climates develop better red color than those in warm climates; thus green varieties are better suited to warmer areas. In most districts, there are usually several satisfactory varieties of proven adaptability. Anticipated market demand and potential competition from other districts should heavily influence decisions regarding additional plantings of these varieties.

For the organic producer, it is important to select varieties that are resistant to anticipated pests and diseases. In parts of the state with spring rainfall, apple scab resistance is very important. Most available apple scab–resistant varieties have also been selected for resistance to powdery mildew, and some to fire blight, which could be important in all growing regions. Early-maturing varieties generally sustain less damage from codling moth. If the fruit can be removed from the tree prior to the next generation of codling moth, sprays or additional applications of pheromones can be eliminated.

Cultivars also differ considerably in their susceptibility to various postharvest disorders. For example, Granny Smith and Red Delicious are very susceptible to storage scald, and Granny Smith, Red

Delicious, and Golden Delicious apples are very susceptible to bitter pit.

There are many new varieties being introduced. Some of these are potentially adaptable to organic production in California because of their excellent fruit characteristics and disease resistance. Since market prices vary so much by variety, there is a trend toward planting new varieties for early production to capture the high prices paid for new varieties. It is worthwhile for growers to have small trial plantings of new varieties for evaluation of adaptability to local conditions. Producing unique varieties with flavor, harvested at the peak of maturity, has always been one of the potential advantages of small-scale apple growers in California. When combined with organic production, prices have been very good (see **Antique and Novelty Varieties** later in this chapter). Reducing pest control costs through the use of disease-resistant varieties could also increase profits.

Most apple varieties require cross-pollination from another variety that blooms at the same time and produces viable pollen. In hedgerow plantings, pollenizers may be planted as solid rows alternating with the main variety or as single trees spread 50 to 100 feet (15 to 30 m) apart in the main variety row. Fewer pollenizers are needed if planted in the tree row because honey bees tend to move down rather than across the rows. Flowering crab apples are commonly used to avoid harvesting difficulties with in-row pollenizers, but many are very susceptible to fire blight.

Principal Varieties. According to a 1995 survey and 1999 estimates of apple acreage made by the California Apple Association, the top ten varieties grown in California, with over 1,000 bearing acres, listed in descending order are Granny Smith, Fuji, Gala, Red Delicious, Golden Delicious, Yellow Newtown, Pink Lady, Rome Beauty, Sommerfeld, and Gravenstein. In the past 10 years, Granny Smith acreage doubled, and there were large increases in plantings of Fuji and Gala in the San Joaquin Valley. However, in the last 4 years, Fuji acreage decreased dramatically due to poor fruit color and susceptibility to fire blight. Acreage of Gala has remained flat, Granny Smith acreage is replacing Fuji, but has declined, and acreage of Pink Lady and Sommerfeld has increased.

The following variety descriptions provide cultural information on the California apple varieties grown organically. Most of the principal varieties grown in California have name recognition and specific reputations in the marketplace, but lack resistance to common diseases.

Granny Smith. This is a very late-maturing variety, green in color, with medium to large, round to slightly conic fruit. It is susceptible to mildew, scab, bitter pit,

fire blight, and water core (especially on young trees). It may scald in storage. As one of the latest-maturing varieties, it is susceptible to codling moth damage through late October. In coastal growing districts it provides adequate annual bearing with only hand thinning.

Fuji. A very late-maturing variety, Fuji has become very popular due to its excellent sweet eating quality, but Central Valley growers have been unable to obtain good color. It is very sensitive to fire blight, scab, water core, and sunburn damage. It is prone to biennial bearing, slow to come into production, and difficult to thin. It is subject to core rots, and, for reasons unknown at this time, fruit harvested later in the season may exhibit internal browning in controlled atmosphere storage in some years. Its late maturity makes it more likely to be attacked by codling moth than earlier varieties.

Gala. An early-maturing, small, summer apple with excellent quality due to its firmness and keeping quality. It is susceptible to fire blight, scab, and European canker. Its earliness provides some advantage for avoiding codling moth damage.

Red Delicious. One of the most widely planted red varieties in the world, Red Delicious is losing favor in the marketplace because of poor flavor caused by harvesting red sports prior to full maturity. It is primarily a fresh-market apple that matures in midseason and can be severely attacked by codling moth. It is susceptible to scab, mildew, and fire blight.

Golden Delicious. This is a widely planted yellow apple of excellent dessert quality. However, it is usually harvested at an immature stage with little flavor, thus earning a poor reputation in the U.S. market. It is self-fruitful and sets a good crop almost every year, but is difficult to thin. Goldens are mature in midseason and very susceptible to codling moth. This variety is susceptible to mildew, scab, bitter pit, and russet, and somewhat susceptible to fire blight.

Yellow Newtown. Grown chiefly in the Watsonville district as a processing apple, this variety is late-maturing and susceptible to stem-end russet, mildew, scab, bitter pit, and internal browning in storage.

Pink Lady. This is a new variety in California. Very late-maturing, and therefore susceptible to heavy codling moth pressure, it is also extremely susceptible to fire blight and apple scab.

Rome Beauty. Red-green striped to solid red, this variety is used mostly for processing and is very susceptible to powdery mildew and scab. Because of its late maturity it is subject to heavy codling moth pressure. It also does not keep well in storage.

Sommerfeld. The real name of this variety is Sensyu. It is an early variety, maturing just after Gala but with better size and a sweetness similar to Fuji. This is not a variety developed from any disease-resistance breeding program, and exact disease susceptibility is unknown at this time.

Gravenstein. This is an early summer apple, primarily grown commercially in the Sebastopol area for processing. It has good fresh-market value because of earliness and name recognition. Its early maturity means that it often avoids the second and third generations of codling moth. It is susceptible to bitter pit, scab, and mildew, does not store well, and bruises easily.

Other Varieties

Jonathan. This variety matures in midseason with excellent quality for both fresh and processing use in coastal growing areas. In Sebastopol, it is harvested prior to the third generation of codling moth. It is highly susceptible to mildew, scab, Jonathan spot, and fire blight.

Braeburn. This apple has a natural, spur-type tree with very high quality fruit and late maturity. It is susceptible to water core, scab, mildew, bitter pit, and fire blight.

Jonagold. A new variety, Jonagold has mid- to late-season maturity. It has excellent eating quality when mature. It is susceptible to scab, mildew, bitter pit, sunburn, and fire blight.

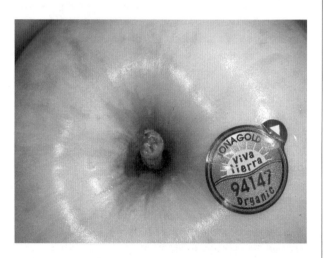

McIntosh. This midseason apple has name recognition but does poorly in California compared to the quality produced on the East Coast. It is susceptible to scab, mildew, and fire blight.

Winesap. An old but still popular late-maturing variety, this apple is best adapted to the mountain districts of California. It can be severely attacked by codling moth. It is susceptible to scab, mildew, and fire blight.

Disease-Resistant Varieties. There have been several scab-resistant varieties developed in breeding programs for the eastern states where this disease is quite

severe due to summer humidity and rain. Some have received limited testing under California growing conditions. In growing districts with extended spring rains, organic growers should experiment with some of these varieties to see how they perform in their orchards.

Enterprise. A large-fruited, late-maturing, dense, crisp variety that stores well. The color is dark red over a yellow green background. This is one of the best of the scab-resistant varieties.

Florina. A promising scab-resistant selection from France, this variety has large, round-oblong, purple-red fruit. It ripens late and has a mixed sweet-tart flavor.

Freedom. This apple is a late season variety with large fruit and mild flavor. It is not completely immune to scab (see color plate 2.1).

Goldrush. A scab-immune selection with Golden Delicious parentage, this fruit is late-maturing, large, firm textured, and tart with an excellent flavor. It stores well (see color plate 2.2).

Pristine. This is a moderate to large, tart, yellow apple, immune to scab and resistant to fire blight and mildew. It matures midseason.

Jonafree. A midseason apple, Jonafree is similar to Jonathan, with soft flesh and uneven coloring.

Liberty. One of the best quality apples of the disease-resistant varieties, Liberty is very productive and requires heavy early thinning to achieve good size. It ripens in midseason, has an attractive red color with some striping, and a good sweet flavor (see color plate 2.3).

Prima. This is an early-maturing, uneven ripening variety of moderate quality.

Priscilla. A late-season variety with small fruit, this apple has soft flesh and mild flavor (see color plate 2.4).

Red Free. This variety matures early. It is a heat sensitive, small-fruited variety that is susceptible to water core, sunburn, and russet.

Williams Pride. A very early-maturing, scab-immune variety, Williams Pride is also resistant to fire blight and mildew. The fruit is medium to large with a round-oblique shape. They have an attractive red-striped color on a green-yellow background (see color plate 2.5).

Early-Maturing Varieties. Most early-maturing varieties do not store well and are not disease resistant. However, Williams Pride is both early and disease resistant. Gala and Gravenstein are the only early varieties extensively planted in California. Some other varieties have acceptable horticultural and culinary qualities, but there is limited experience with them in California. Early varieties (approximate ripening dates in parentheses) that may be of interest are the following:

Anna (July1)
Vista Bell (July 1)
Jerseymac (July 10)
Dorset Golden (July 10)
Paulared (July 15)
Akane (August 1)
Mollygold (August 1)

Sunrise (August 1)
Williams Pride (August 1)
Ginger Gold (August 10)
Sansa (August 10)
Jonamac (August 15)
Summer Red (August 15)

Antique and Novelty Varieties. The antique and novelty apple varieties have name recognition in the marketplace and have been grown historically, but they have generally been replaced by other varieties because of color, alternate bearing, disease susceptibility, or other considerations. Many have promise as specialty varieties with unique flavor. Varieties that have been grown by smaller organic growers have been produced with more attention to detail, especially harvest maturity, thereby providing better flavored fruit. Organic growers have often taken advantage of this difference in flavor due to maturity and small-scale handling. This has created an increased interest in organically grown, nontraditional varieties with good flavor for niche markets.

Antique Varieties for Trial

Arkansas Black	Northern Spy
Baldwin	Red Golden
Black Twig	Sierra Beauty
Cox's Orange Pippin	Staymen Winesap
Empire	Wagner
E. Spitzenburg	Winter Banana

New or Novelty Varieties for Trial

Arlet	Golden Supreme
Cameo	Hawaii
Carousel	Honeycrisp
Elstar	Pink Parfait
Fortune	Pink Pearl
Gala Supreme	Senshu

Tree Nutrition and Fertilization

In general, any material applied to the soil or crop as a fertility or growth enhancement agent in organic apples must be derived from natural sources as defined by California (and federal) regulations. Included are amendments derived from animal sources (for example, manures and manure products, composts, fishmeals and emulsions, and blood and bone meals).

Plant-derived products include kelp meal and sprays, cottonseed meal, mulches, and cover crop biomass. Mineral nutrient sources (lime sulfur, copper, gypsum, limestone, elemental sulfur, Bordeaux [copper hydroxide], dolomite, rock phosphate, oystershell lime, potassium sulfate, calcium chloride, and so on) must be mined or otherwise naturally occurring; they cannot be synthetically manufactured. Manufactured micronutrients (zinc sulfate, iron compounds) may only be used if a specific deficiency for that nutrient has been diagnosed. As with any applied materials or questionable practice, it is the grower's responsibility to consult state (and federal) lists of allowed products, then to check with their certifier for additional compliance standards, if necessary.

Specific recommendations for fertilization of organically grown apple trees cannot be made because of variations in soil, moisture, and temperature within and among districts in California. However, multiyear studies in California indicate that it is not difficult to provide adequate nutrients to apple trees under organic management.

Annual average nutrient removal by apple fruit in a 20-ton (18-metric ton) crop is 29 pounds per acre (32 kg/ha) of nitrogen, 4 pounds per acre (4.5 kg/ha) of phosphorous, and 56 pounds per acre (63 kg/ha) of potassium. Typically, a legume (bell bean/vetch) cover crop plus 2 or more tons per acre of chicken manure-based compost are incorporated in the spring each year (see color plate 2.6). This is enough for the entire tree and crop needs for the season, including micronutrients. Supplemental foliar applications of kelp, fishmeal, or compost tea have not demonstrated any benefit to apple trees.

Nitrogen is usually the only element that needs to be added to the orchard on a regular basis because it is used in large quantities, and most other nutrients are available naturally from the soil. Generally, mature apple trees need between 50 and 100 pounds per acre (56 and 112 kg/ha) of actual nitrogen per year. Common ways for organic growers to add nitrogen to the orchard are through applications of manures, composts, dried blood meal, feather meal, and by using leguminous cover crops. Nitrogen-fixing cover crops tilled into the soil have been demonstrated to produce between 50 and 150 pounds (23 and 68 kg) of nitrogen in one season (see the **Cover Crop Selection and Management** section of this chapter).

Because nitrogen-containing materials and cover crops break down into amino acids and subsequently into mineral nitrogen (NO_3 and NH_4) for plant uptake more slowly than conventional fertilizers, applications should be planned in advance. The low concentration and form of nitrogen in organic materials may require several months for microorganisms to convert it to the mineral form available to plants. Consequently, available nitrogen is more likely to come from an application made the previous year and stored in the soil. Therefore, annual applications should be made to maintain adequate levels over time.

In high rainfall areas, fall and winter applications of organic nitrogen-containing fertilizers should be avoided to limit significant nitrogen loss from denitrification and leaching, leading to environmental contamination. Denitrification is the volatilization of nitrogen into the air under low oxygen conditions (saturated soil). Under these circumstances, early spring applications provide the greatest nitrogen use efficiency.

If necessary, composts or dried, concentrated forms of organic fertilizers such as feather meal, blood meal, fish waste, and so on can be applied around the root zone to boost growth, especially in young trees. These forms of nitrogen will still take several weeks in warm weather or several months in cool weather to provoke a response in the trees.

Importing large quantities of materials from off-site can be expensive due to processing and hauling costs. Finished composts should be evaluated for major nutrients on a dry weight basis in order to calculate appropriate application rates for the orchard system. In general, application rates in organic apples have ranged from 1 to 5 tons per acre (1 to 5.5 metric tons/ha) in fall or spring applications, depending upon the nutrient values of the compost or fertilizer meals. For example, 1 ton (908 kg) of compost with a nitrogen analysis of 2 percent supplies 40 pounds per acre (45 kg/ha) of actual nitrogen.

The use of uncomposted manures is restricted in California organic production, both by state regulations and certification agencies. This is due to potential nitrogen leaching during the winter and contamination of fruit with *E. coli* bacteria.

The best way to monitor nitrogen and other nutrient levels of apple trees is by leaf analysis each July. At that time of year, the spur leaf nitrogen content should be at least 2 percent but not more than 2.4 percent. See table 2.1.

Phosphorus deficiency is very rare in California's apple trees because of the phosphorous naturally present in most soils. Rock phosphate or bone meal are both organically acceptable forms of phosphorous, and most composts contain some available phosphorous. Little or no reaction will occur in tree growth or performance if phosphorous is added to soils unless leaf analysis strongly indicates a deficiency. Phosphorous, however, is often applied to improve the growth of leguminous cover crops.

Potassium deficiency is fairly common in California. Organic growers can correct the requirement for potassium with a heavy application of mined potassium sulfate. Potassium is strongly adsorbed by clay particles in the soil, so potassium fertilizers must be placed close to tree roots in order to gain a response in the trees. Generally, 750 to 2,000 pounds per acre (840 to 2,240 kg/ha) of potassium sulfate are trenched into the soil at a depth of about 6 inches (15 cm) at the drip line of the trees or applied to the surface in the fall. The higher rate is used on heavier clay soils, and the lower rate is used on sandy or lighter textured soils. In drip-irrigated orchards, applications can be made directly under emitters at about 20 percent of the trenched rates.

Deficiencies of micronutrients such as zinc, boron, calcium, manganese, copper, and magnesium are not very common. It is usually necessary to combine visual observation of symptoms and known characteristics of specific deficiencies with a leaf tissue analysis in order to properly diagnose these micronutrient deficiencies.

When micronutrient deficiencies occur, they are normally treated with foliar mineral sprays. Foliar sprays containing a wide range of nutrients derived from organic sources such as compost tea, fish emulsion, and sea kelp can be used to correct deficiencies. Because the concentration of any one micronutrient in a spray is very low, they generally require numerous applications in order to be effective. When applied on a regular basis to correct a specifically identified deficiency, sprays will usually turn leaves a deeper green color and have demonstrated effects on growth, yield, return bloom, and fruit size.

In most cases, when a deficiency has been identified through laboratory leaf tissue analysis, current organic laws allow nonorganic forms of micronutrients to be used to correct the deficiency. Generally, one application is all that is needed. For more details on this subject, see **Tree Nutrition and Fertilization** in *Commercial Apple Growing in California* (ANR Publication 2456, 1992). If micronutrient deficiencies occur or are suspected, consult the local University of California Cooperative Extension Farm Advisor for help in

Table 2.1. Critical nutrient levels of apple spur leaves sampled in July.

Nutrient	Deficient below	Sufficient	Excess over
Nitrogen	1.9%	2.0 – 2.4%	2.4%
Phosphorus	—	0.1 – 0.3%	—
Potassium	1.0%	>1.2%	—
Magnesium	—	>0.25%	—
Calcium	—	>1.0%	—
Chloride	—	—	0.3%
Zinc	—	>18 ppm	—
Boron	20 ppm	25 – 70 ppm	100 ppm
Manganese	—	>20 ppm	—
Copper	—	>4 ppm	—

Source: Commercial Apple Growing in California (ANR Publication 2456, 1992), p.14.

evaluating the problem and advice on organically acceptable materials.

Fruit Thinning

With good bloom, it takes approximately 10 percent of the blossoms to set apples for a full crop. Under adverse weather conditions or if bloom is sparse, growers ensure an adequate set by planting pollenizer trees within the main variety to provide pollen through synchronized bloom and by bringing in hives of honey bees (2 hives/acre [5 hives/ha]) to make sure pollen is transferred between blossoms. Setting too many apples and then thinning excess fruit by hand is preferable to not setting enough apples.

Alternate bearing, the term used to describe a heavy crop one year and a light crop the next year, is caused by alternate bloom. In years with heavy bloom, many small fruit are set. During the 30- to 45-day period between full bloom and small fruit stage, the tree also produces flower initials in the spurs for the following year. The large crop of tiny fruit on the tree produces hormones that send a chemical message to the developing spurs and flower buds not to initiate flowers the following year. Consequently, next year's bloom is light, fewer fruit have an opportunity to set, and crops are lighter, as well.

To prevent alternate bearing, hand thinning is usually done when the fruit reaches ½ to 1 inch in diameter. The fruit are easier to remove and space when they are larger than this, but the most effective way to prevent alternate bearing and increase final fruit size is to thin the tiny fruits during the same period when flowers are initiated for the following year, that is, within 30 to 45 days after full bloom (see color plate 2.7).

Estimates of hand thinning costs for an acre of mature trees can range from $500 to $1,500. The cost is higher for large trees because ladders must be used.

Hand thinning is accomplished by removing the small fruit and leaving one to two fruits per spur (spaced 7 to 8 inches [18 to 20.5 cm] apart), depending on the total set of the crop, variety, and growing conditions. Thin for size as well as proper spacing. Save the largest fruit because size differences present during thinning will still be present at harvest. To achieve the greatest number of large fruit, leave two large fruit together and thin smaller ones rather than leave a large one and a small one. However, it has been observed that thinning to one fruit per cluster so that fruit are not touching can reduce codling moth damage because spray coverage is better. In addition, codling moth larvae often enter where the fruit are touching and sometimes move from one fruit to the next if they touch.

ORCHARD FLOOR MANAGEMENT

The primary objective in managing the orchard floor in most organic systems is to provide natural sustainable fertility to the trees. This usually involves the use of cover crops and the application of organic fertilizers to increase organic matter and provide a steady release of available nutrients to the trees as the organic matter breaks down. Many choices need to be made regarding the type of irrigation system to use in conjunction with a mowed or tilled cover crop, as well as the choice of the specific type of cover crop to grow.

The orchard floor is also managed to control weed competition and provide access to the trees for harvest and spray applications. Equipment needs, costs, and timing considerations for these operations are important. Soil type and drainage influence ease of access into the orchard and potential for soil compaction. Growers need to know about their specific soil characteristics and the interaction with rootstocks, climate, irrigation, and fertility in order to manage the orchard floor profitably.

Weed Control

Weed control is one of the biggest challenges in organic apple production due to the high costs of alternative methods when compared to herbicides. Organic weed control methods include the use of living cover crops, cultivation to uproot or cut weeds, mulches to smother weeds, and flamers to burn or "cook" weeds.

Removal of competition with tree growth is important in all orchards but especially significant in the first few years of young orchards. Weed competition at the base of first-, second-, and third-year trees can reduce growth by as much as two-thirds and reduce the bearing surface development by several years. Trees (especially those on dwarfing rootstocks) that have been stunted are very difficult, if not impossible, to bring back to a good economically productive state. Factors such as tree age, irrigation system, and weed type can have an important influence on weed impact in an orchard.

Any plant, even a cover crop planted by the orchardist, can be a weed if it is competing with tree growth and productivity. The worst weeds are perennials that vigorously compete with tree growth during the active growing season of the tree and fruit. Winter weed growth is not a problem for dormant trees if it is suppressed prior to resumption of tree growth in the spring. Weeds on the orchard floor during the dormant season can even help reduce erosion and improve soil tilth and orchard accessibility.

Cultivation. Mechanical cultivation is expensive because it requires a mid-sized tractor with specialized equipment, repeated passes, and more labor, especially for the control of weeds within the tree rows. Orchards are cultivated to

- reduce weeds that compete for water and nutrients

- facilitate subsequent orchard operations, such as irrigation, harvesting, and orchard brush removal or spraying

- incorporate cover crops and fertilizers

- prepare seedbeds for cover crops

- aid in the infiltration of water where operations have caused compaction

Cultivation should not be any deeper or more frequent than is necessary to accomplish these objectives. It does not reduce water loss except by killing weeds that use water. Unnecessary cultivation, especially when the soil is wet, not only increases operating costs but may also cause soil damage. Care should be taken not to spread plant parts of perennial weeds like bermudagrass, field bindweed, and Johnsongrass through cultivation.

Perennial grass-sod culture, resident vegetation, or planted cover crops can be used between rows in apple orchards. They offer the advantages of erosion control, improved water infiltration, lowered cost, ease of maintenance, and better access in winter. However, such plant covers may harbor insect and rodent pests, require additional water and nitrogen, and compete with trees.

To minimize these drawbacks, orchard floor plant cover located directly under the trees is usually cultivated mechanically using specially designed equipment that goes around the tree trunks, or it is hand hoed. Vegetation between rows is mowed or flailed as needed but can be cultivated as well to save water in nonirrigated orchards or to open soils that tend to seal over time without cultivation.

Specialized equipment used for cultivation within the tree row usually consists of an articulating blade or rotating head that is triggered by a switch. When near the tree trunk, the blade or head moves around the trunk to avoid injuring the tree. Equipment options include the French plow, triggered rototiller, triggered cutting blade, and triggered spinning heads with cultivation spikes. Whatever cultivation technique is used, it is essential to avoid injuring trees or roots. Such injuries can weaken trees permanently and lead to disease.

Mulches. Organic mulches can effectively control weeds, retain moisture, provide a sustained low level of nutrition for the trees, and in some cases reduce root rot. Many municipal waste collection programs have green waste materials that are a combination of prunings, grass clippings, and ground lumber.

Unfortunately, most organic mulches for weed control are usually only practical in small-scale operations because of the high cost of materials and hauling fees. Recent research indicates that mulch chips need to be 3 to 4 inches (7.5 to 10 cm) deep to effectively control weeds, while just 1 inch of mulch actually encourages weed problems. This type of deep coverage requires a great deal of material—200 cubic yards per acre of organic mulch is needed for an orchard spaced 8 by 16 feet (2.4 by 4.9 m), and a mulch applied to a strip 6 feet (1.8 m) wide and 4 inches (10 cm) deep under the tree. There is also considerable cost in application within the tree row if done by hand. Modified side-discharge livestock feed wagons have been used to apply mulch in larger-scale operations.

An alternative to hauling in an organic mulch is to grow it in the orchard in the middles between tree rows, cut it, and move it into the rows under the trees for weed control. Specialized mowing equipment has been developed to efficiently relocate mulch material. Typically, a low-nitrogen, high-biomass grass cover crop such as one of the cereal grains is grown for this purpose because it will not break down as rapidly as leguminous cover crops. However, organic mulches sometimes provide favorable habitat for rodents such as meadow mice that can cause tree trunk injury (see chapter 3).

Fabric mulches are another option for in-row weed control (see color plate 2.8). These mulches control 100 percent of the weeds, allow for rapid water penetration from sprinklers or emitters, and provide a clean surface for leaf removal to reduce apple scab inoculum. Initial costs are high, but some of the materials can last up to 10 years, making the investment comparable to conventional herbicide costs.

There are many different brands of woven weed control fabric. Some have very high tensile strength (160 lb by 110 lb) and contain special UV inhibitors for extended outdoor life. They are usually guaranteed for several years and have lasted even longer in some experimental orchards. These fabric mulches can be applied in a 3-foot (0.9-m) strip on each side of the tree row or at planting as a 6-foot (1.8-m) band cleared for the tree trunks. It is typically pinned down with 6-inch (15-cm) wire hoop stakes. For an orchard with a tree spacing of 8 feet by 16 feet (2.4 by 4.9 m), the cost per acre is approximately $730 for polypropylene fabric and another $200 per acre for stakes and the labor to pin it down.

Flamers. Technology made available in the last few years has greatly improved the effectiveness of propane burners as a weed control method. The system requires one or two large metal flame tubes to release heat at the base of tree trunks. The flamer tubes are connected to propane tanks with valves to adjust the heat level and a safety switch. Propane burners are pulled through the orchard at a speed that "cooks" emerging weeds before they develop much size or vigor. Flaming may require several passes and weeds should be flamed before reaching 2 inches (5 cm) in height. This is especially true for grasses, which are tolerant and more difficult to control because the growing point is low within the plant. Care must be taken not to injure young trees or to damage irrigation equipment or trellis materials. Dry weeds or leaves can create a fire hazard, and workers must use care in handling propane flamers to avoid injury.

Cover Crop Selection and Management

Choosing a cover crop depends on the orchard location, irrigation system, pest control considerations, and fertility needs. Fortunately, apples require somewhat less nitrogen compared to some other tree crops, and research has shown that it is relatively easy to provide adequate nutrition with leguminous cover crops. For orchards with grass cover crops, nitrogen must be supplied through application of some type of organic fertilizer such as compost, blood meal, or feather meal.

Spring frosts can be more severe in cover-cropped orchards compared to clean-cultivated ground. Moist, black soil absorbs heat during the day and releases it at night to create 2° to 3°F warmer temperatures. Permanent sod can also keep the orchard cooler and more humid in the summer leading to potential disease problems but may provide habitat for beneficial insect predators and aid in pest control. Conversely, some pests that attack apples may find harbor in a cover crop and increase pest damage.

There are many reasons for growing cover crops in apple orchards, but there are also situations where a cover crop or specific type of cover crop can be detrimental to economic crop production.

Positive Attributes of Cover Crops

Add nitrogen	Manage excess vigor
Add organic matter	Provide habitat for
Provide winter access	beneficials
Enhance water	Compete with noxious
penetration	weeds
Reduce erosion	Moderate temperature
	Look attractive

Potential Problems with Cover Crops

Use water	Provide habitat for
Invade like weeds	insects and diseases
Increase vertebrate	Increase frost risk
pest problems	Seal certain soils
Cost to establish and	Look unattractive
maintain	

Selection. In organic apple orchards, cover crops supply organic matter that leads to soil aggregation, increased aeration, and a slow release of nutrients. The primary use, however, is to add nitrogen to the soil since nitrogen may be a limiting factor. For this reason, most growers use nitrogen-fixing legumes or a blend of legumes and grasses. But the decision of what cover crop mix to use depends on the individual orchard and the management practices in place.

In general, organic growers should avoid extremely aggressive perennial clovers, especially in young orchards, since they are difficult or impossible to control. These include white clovers (including Dutch, Ladino, and Wild White), narrowleaf and broadleaf trefoil, and strawberry clovers (including Salina, O'Connor, and Palestine).

The main factors to consider when selecting a particular cover crop species or mix are costs and benefits, irrigation method, tillage practices, soil type, soil depth, tree nutritional status, and especially, local weather conditions and frost concerns. Winter temperatures and rainfall will have a significant influence on the success of certain cover crops. The choice and performance of cover crops often depend on site-specific factors, so they should first be tested in a few rows before planting large acreages. Understanding the basic cover crop types and management strategies can greatly improve the chances for using these inputs successfully.

Management Systems. Cover crops can simply be resident vegetation in the orchard. However, many growers like to plant specific cover crops for nitrogen fixation, increased biomass, or better habitat for beneficial insects. There are four typical management systems that incorporate the use of various types of cover crops: (1) year-round clean cultivation, (2) winter cover-summer cultivation, (3) winter cover-summer mowed, and (4) mowed permanent cover.

Year-Round Clean Cultivation. No cover crops are used in clean-cultivated orchards, which are tilled almost all year to control weeds when using movable sprinkler systems and to provide the ditches and basins for flood or furrow irrigation. Clean cultivation is not common in organic apple production. It may save water by removing plants that compete with apple trees for water when infiltration is not a problem. Complete weed control also eliminates competition for nutrients, thereby enhancing tree growth. A tradeoff is that bare soil can have greater evaporation losses compared to a surface covered with some dead, dry vegetation.

There are disadvantages to year-round clean cultivation. Frequent cultivation can increase soil compaction and lead to water infiltration problems and the need to rip the soil more often to break up the compacted layer. If soils are worked when wet, soil structure is broken down, decreasing soil surface friability and water penetration. Year-round clean cultivation usually leads to very low organic matter content in the soil. The soil may require the liberal application of organic matter such as compost or manures to maintain soil tilth and nutrition, which can be costly.

Winter Cover–Summer Cultivation. High biomass cover crop species and mixes can produce large amounts of organic matter and can be used in tilled orchards to naturally gain maximum nitrogen potential. These mixes usually contain large-seeded grasses and legumes that are easy to grow. Sown each fall and disked in the spring, they are referred to as *green manure* cover crops or winter cover crops. Green manure cover crops should be disked before the soil dries excessively. This enables the disk to penetrate the soil, especially in orchards with drip systems or microsprinklers where the cover crop and soil cannot be irrigated.

In sprinkler-, furrow-, or flood-irrigated orchards, the grower may need to mow the cover early in the season (prior to cultivation) in order to facilitate water flow and coverage. Removing the cover crop and weeds is an important consideration with drip emitters or mini-sprinklers within the row. This can be accomplished with in-row cultivation equipment, flamers, mulching, or mowing. Irrigation tubing must be suspended above the ground to avoid contact with the heat from the flamer or the tines of the in-row cultivator.

Seed and farming supply companies offer two basic types of green manure mixes: pure legume and legume-grass blends. Pure legume mixes usually consist of bell beans, field peas, and vetch, and are used to add a large amount of rapidly available nitrogen to the soil when incorporated. Bell beans produce vigorous, upright growth (see color plate 2.9). However, they cannot be mowed closely, which may be a concern in areas prone to spring frost.

Field peas are also vigorous; those most commonly planted as cover crops include Austrian Winter and Magnus. Austrian Winter pea is dormant during cold weather, producing nearly all its biomass during the spring. However, it will usually produce as much biomass as most other legumes if allowed to grow through the spring. Magnus grows rapidly through the winter and matures earlier than Austrian Winter. It is a better choice in orchards disked early in the spring. Field peas are shallow rooted and subject to drought in sandy soils.

Vetches are frequently used in legume blends, but may twine up trees or sprinklers if planted too close to them. In addition, if allowed to reseed they may become a weed problem within the rows. Lana woolly-pod is one of the most vigorous vetches in the spring; it flowers and matures earlier than purple vetch. Common vetch has extrafloral nectaries on the stipules that may provide nectar to beneficial insects. Cahaba White vetch has been shown to suppress root knot nematodes. If these vetches are used, they need to be planted 2 to 3 feet (0.6 to 0.9 m) away from trees, or some hand-hoeing will have to be done to remove plant material growing up into the trees.

Berseem clover is rarely sown in orchards, but may have some value to growers seeking to add large amounts of nitrogen to the soil. It grows through the spring and early summer and flowers in June. Highly palatable, it responds well to mowing and grazing.

Various legume-grass blends are also available for cover cropping. Adding grasses such as barley, oats, or cereal rye to a mix imparts several benefits. The fibrous roots of grasses greatly enhance soil tilth and water penetration. Grasses also absorb excess nitrogen from the soil, improving the nitrogen fixing ability of the legumes. In addition, grasses provide structural support for the twining vetches and peas. Typical blends often consist of bell beans, vetch, peas, and oats or barley.

Barley-vetch or oat-vetch blends are relatively inexpensive and are a popular choice for growers. If you choose one of these blends, be aware that grasses may reduce or delay the availability to the trees of nitrogen from the legumes, especially if the grasses are planted at higher rates. For adequate nitrogen availability, grasses should not exceed approximately 10 to 15 percent of the mix. Grasses do, however, add more organic matter to the soil and take longer to degrade, thus helping to maintain higher organic matter levels in the soil.

Rotate to different cover crops every 2 to 3 years to avoid the buildup of diseases that can reduce the biomass of the planting just as you would in any annual system. Bell beans and fava beans in particular have suffered in wet seasons when used as the cover crop in the same orchard without rotation. Cover crop mixes offer some benefit in biodiversity as conditions change from year to year and favor one species over another.

Early fall cover crop plantings (September through October) may require irrigation to achieve germination and early growth, but early plantings provide much more total growth and biomass than later plantings and can be tilled earlier in the spring. Winter plantings (November through January) produce almost all of their biomass in the spring. When late planting is the only option, choose a cover crop that will germinate under cooler soil conditions like the vetches (Lana, common, and purple) and large-seeded grasses.

Winter Cover–Summer Mowed. With the increasing trend toward nontillage, many organic growers sow winter annual species that reseed and die in the spring, regenerating each fall with either irrigation or rainfall. This system is easily adapted to flood irrigation with permanent or semipermanent berms, movable sprinklers, and solid set sprinklers, or with minisprinklers and drip emitters when lines are suspended in order to flame or cultivate within the row. For ease of maintenance, these cover crops should only be planted between rows and not within the tree row so that they do not become a weed control problem.

The benefit of this type of system is that these species use less water than perennial cover crop species, often choke out unwanted annual weeds, offer habitat for beneficial insects, and provide adequate fertility with natural reseeding. Such species include subterranean and other annual clovers, burr medic, Blando brome, and Zorro fescue.

Blando brome is often used for erosion control. Zorro fescue is very expensive and is used mostly on hillsides, serpentine, low fertility soils, or where initial erosion control is required on cleared land. These grasses should not be used alone in organic orchards unless adequate nitrogen is available or applied. If not replanted or if neglected, reseeding cover crop species may in time simply become minor components of the ground cover. Replanting cover crops every three or four years can ensure dominance by these species. Some grasses are hard to seed with many seeding implements. For example, Zorro fescue should be coated by the supplier if a standard grain drill is used. Small areas can, however, be hand spread and lightly incorporated with a harrow or mulching ring roller.

Burr medic is well adapted to California's climate, grows well in neutral to high-pH soils, and is occasionally a major component of resident vegetation. It effectively reseeds even under close mowing, and, because of its high percentage of hard seed, it usually reestablishes well even when tillage is used. Subterranean clover, or subclover, usually performs best in acid to neutral soils low in nitrogen. Early-maturing varieties, frequently used on rangeland, include Nungarin and Dalkeith. It is advisable to plant a mixture of varieties with differing maturity dates to help ensure long-term maintenance of the stand.

Mowed Permanent Cover. Perennial grasses and legumes provide a permanent cover that offers traction year-round, as well as dust control and ease of management. Equipment and operating costs can be lower compared to cultivation because smaller horsepower tractors can be used and speed of travel is faster. Soil compaction is usually less problematic with sod or perennial clover. Surface sealing of soil is not a problem with permanent cover crop systems, but some soils can have slow percolation due to the surface plant material and may need to be cultivated periodically to enhance water infiltration. However, in most cases perennial plant cover improves infiltration. Sod should be kept moist. If allowed to dry, it is often difficult to wet because of the hydrophobic nature of the organic material and causes water to run off.

Permanent cover uses 20 to 30 percent more water than other types of cover cropping and requires a sprinkler system to maintain the row middles during the dry summer months. Drip and minisprinkler systems do not provide sufficient watering for permanent cover crops. The best irrigation system for permanent sod is permanent or movable sprinklers, although controlling the cover crop around permanent sprinklers can become a problem and may be costly if control by hand becomes necessary.

Perennial clovers, such as white and strawberry, are low growing and add nitrogen but are invasive and compete with trees for water. Birdsfoot trefoil, a legume, is slow to establish but forms a low-growing, dense cover. Some clovers may increase populations of detrimental nematode species and gophers.

Vigorous perennial grasses such as bermudagrass, Berber wheatgrass, tall fescue, and perennial ryegrass can be problematic in organic orchards since they strongly compete for both water and nitrogen. Lower-growing, fine-leafed fescues may be appropriate in some cases because they use less nitrogen and water. Nevertheless, extra nitrogen in the form of manures or composts must be applied for their growth.

General Cover Crop Management Strategies and Considerations

Planting. Winter annual and perennial cover crops perform best when sown by mid-October but can usually be successfully grown if planted by mid-November. In general, lower seeding rates can be used for early seeding, and higher rates should be used for later seeding.

Good seedbed preparation is essential, especially with small-seeded species. Establishing small-seeded cover crops in years with little fall rain is very difficult without irrigation, especially in sandy soils. Seed early (October) in areas that are prone to erosion to provide some cover before winter rains.

To prepare a seedbed for cover crops, cultivate to eliminate weeds that are present in the orchard and provide a fine soil particle size for the seeds to germinate. This may be accomplished with 2 to 3 diskings or with a spader or rototiller. Seedbed preparation need only be 2 to 3 inches (5 to 7.5 cm) deep; deeper tillage is not necessary and may require rolling prior to seeding if large clods are created. Small seeds should be planted at a shallow depth of approximately ½ to 1 inch (1.25 to 2.5 cm) whereas large-seeded cover crops can be sown up to 2 inches (5 cm) deep. With a good seedbed, broadcast seeders can be used, followed by a harrow and ring roller or just a mulching ring roller.

Another option is to use seed drills that are typically used in sowing grains. These can usually be modified to plant several different sizes and shapes of seeds. The advantage of using a seed drill is that it eliminates the need to till the soil to develop a fine seedbed. Most establishments that sell seeds also rent seed drills.

Legume seeds should be inoculated with nitrogen-fixing *Rhizobium* bacteria to ensure nitrogen fixation. Small-seeded legumes are usually preinoculated; large-seeded legumes (bell beans, vetch, and peas) must be inoculated by the grower, at least the first time they are sown. Use approximately 8 ounces (227 g) of inoculant per 100 pounds (45 kg) of seed. The wet method is the most reliable—a slurry of inoculum and adhesive is added to the seed, which is then allowed to dry before planting. The dry inoculant can also simply be layered with seed in the hopper when planted with a drill; for broadcasting, inoculant must be applied with the wet method. Inoculant and inoculated seed should be kept out of direct sunlight, so broadcast seed should be incorporated as soon as possible.

Mowing. Because cover crops can increase frost hazard, they are often mowed in late winter. Bell beans, peas, and tall-growing green manure blends can be killed in spring if mowed close to the ground, so they should not be used in areas prone to frost, or they should be tilled in prior to frost season. For continued growth, vetch should be mowed high—no lower than 8 to 10 inches (20.5 to 25.5 cm). Clover mixes should be mowed in late winter to suppress tall weeds and encourage spreading. Subclover and burr medic can usually reseed even under fairly close mowing (3 to 5 inches [7.5 to 12.5 cm]). Crimson and rose clovers flower above the foliage and therefore must not be mowed until after seed mature in late March. In irrigated orchards, some cover crops must be mowed several times during the season.

Mowing some cover crops while in bloom can help force bees to visit the targeted blossoms of the apple trees. Conversely, if thrips are a problem, they can move into apple blossoms from cover crop flowers, causing russeting and scarring of fruit.

Nutrition. As with trees, soil fertility is critical to cover crop production. Legumes fix nitrogen, so nitrogen fertilizers should not be applied to the soil before or dur-

---

How to Calculate Nitrogen Input from a Cover Crop

1. Cut and weigh the fresh cover crop from 16 square feet (4 by 4 feet). Samples should be free of dew.

2. Multiply the fresh weight in pounds by the factor for that particular cover crop (given below) to estimate the pounds of nitrogen per acre contained in the cover crop.

3. Repeat this sampling 5 to 10 times throughout the field, depending on its uniformity. Average your results.

Factors

Lana woollypod	16
Purple vetch	16
Bell beans	10
Berseem clover	13
Cowpeas	12

Source: Covercrops for California Agriculture (ANR Publication 21471, 1989).

---

ing their growth, as this limits the amount fixed by the legumes. Legumes require adequate sulfur and phosphorus for good growth. Annual grasses require nitrogen additions if grown alone. In general, grasses predominate on highly fertile sites, while legumes usually grow best in soils with low nitrogen content. Poor performing, solid legume plantings (especially clovers and medics) that are overtaken by grasses and mustards may be the result of high soil nitrogen.

In general, vetches and peas can fix far more nitrogen than clovers and medics. A green manure cover crop disked in April can add 150 pounds per acre (168 kg/ha) or more of nitrogen (see color plate 2.10). Berseem clover can potentially fix 200 or more pounds per acre (224 or more kg/ha) of nitrogen if mowed periodically and disked in late spring.

Nitrogen utilization by mowed cover crops is not the same as when cover crops are tilled in. When residues are mowed and allowed to remain on the soil surface, a portion of the nitrogen will volatilize into the atmosphere. With about 80 percent of the nitrogen in leguminous cover crops contained in the aboveground portion, volatilization losses can be high—perhaps as much as half. Nontillage clovers and medics may add only about 30 to 40 pounds per acre (34 to 45 kg/ha) of nitrogen. Late-growing clovers that remain in the orchard after deciduous trees leaf out in the spring will also fix less nitrogen during that period due to tree shading and in-row weed management.

Specific Cover Crop Characteristics and Suggested Seeding Rates

Mowed Perennial Grasses

Bermudagrass. This crop competes with trees for water and nutrients and can become an invasive weed that is difficult to control. It tolerates drought and traffic, prevents erosion, and grows best in warm locations, but is not recommended for organic orchards. (40 Bu sprigs/acre)

Buffalograss. This is a low growing (4 to 8 in [10 to 20.5 cm]), drought tolerant, stoloniferous, warm season grass from the Midwest. It is not as aggressive as bermudagrass and has no rhizomes. It should be planted from seed in early spring. In Oregon and the eastern United States it is dormant in summer without water but will regreen when irrigated or with winter rains. (20 to 40 lb/acre [22 to 45 kg/ha])

Tall Fescue. Tall fescue competes with trees for water and nutrients but can tolerate the abuse of orchard traffic. A clumping type grass that does not produce stolons or rhizomes, tall fescue only fills in bare spots if reseeded. There are several varieties, from old Fawn to dwarf Mustangs and double dwarf Mini-Mustang. Tall fescue is quite drought tolerant but dies if it does not receive some summer irrigation. (12 to 15 lb/acre [13 to 17 kg/ha])

Perennial Ryegrass. A lawn type, clumping turf that does best in cooler climates, perennial ryegrass uses large amounts of water and dies if not irrigated frequently in the summer. It requires little nitrogen input. (6 to 10 lb/acre [7 to 11 kg/ha])

Kentucky Bluegrass. This lawn type turf does best in cooler climates. It uses large amounts of water and dies if not summer irrigated. It spreads by stolons and requires high nitrogen input to do well. (2 to 3 lb/acre [2.2 to 3.4 kg/ha])

Fine Fescues. Creeping red fescue, hard fescue, and sheep fescue are very shade tolerant grasses. They produce stolons that creep into open areas, usually reach 10 inches (25.5 cm) in height, and then flop over. They require nitrogen fertilization and frequent irrigation. (6 to 8 lb/acre [7 to 9 kg/ha])

Mowed Winter Annual Grasses (See color plate 2.11.)

Zorro. This is a short growing (12 to 18 in [30.5 to 46 cm]), very fine, bladed grass that reseeds well. It matures seed early in the spring and therefore does not use much water. It is best to mow after seeds are mature. (10 to 20 lb/acre [11 to 22 kg/ha])

Blando Brome. Also known as soft chess, this is an intermediate height (16 to 24 in [41 to 61 cm]) grass more aggressive than Zorro. It matures early and uses little water. (6 to 12 lb/acre [7 to 13 kg/ha])

Annual Ryegrass. This is a very aggressive, easy to establish grass that matures late and uses considerable water. It is very good for areas requiring winter erosion control as the primary consideration. (10 to 20 lb/acre [11 to 22 kg/ha])

Grain, Barley, or Oats. These cover crops grow 3 feet (0.9 m) tall and compete well with weeds. They produce abundant biomass, which is variable by variety. When cut and moved to the tree row, these are the best choices for mulching between trees to reduce summer weeds. (60 to 90 lb/acre [67 to 101 kg/ha])

Mowed Winter Annual Legumes

Subterranean Clover. Many varieties exist. This low-growing (8 to 12 in [20.5 to 30.5 cm]) clover not only tolerates mowing but also successfully competes with weeds when mowed. It reseeds readily, matures early in spring, and uses little water. Plant several varieties with different maturity times to assure a good stand. (12 to 20 lb/acre [13 to 22 kg/ha])

Rose Clover. This low-growing (12 in [30.5 cm]) clover sets seed early and uses little water. Several varieties exist. (9 to 12 lb/acre [10 to 13 kg/ha])

Crimson Clover. This clover grows about 18 inches (45.5 cm) tall and is slightly more aggressive than subterranean or rose clover. It matures later and reseeds best under high moisture conditions. (9 to 12 lb/acre [10 to 13 kg/ha])

Burr Clover. This native medic clover can be mowed short. It reseeds early and uses little water. (6 to 10 lb/acre [7 to 11 kg/ha])

Berseem Clover. This 14- to 18-inch (35.5- to 45.5-cm) clover can be mowed several times to produce continued forage. It needs more water than winter annual clovers like subterranean. (9 to 12 lb/acre [10 to 13 kg/ha])

Tilled Annual Grasses

Ryegrass, Cereal Oats, Barley, or Cereal Rye. These varieties produce a large biomass. Plant in October and November and irrigate. Then till in prior to seed maturity. These cover crops require the addition of nitrogen for a good stand. If mowed high in February, regrowth occurs for a second mowing in March or April. Cereal rye is very effective in sandy soils. (ryegrass: 10 to 20 lb/acre [11 to 22 kg/ha] or 50 to 60 lb/acre [56 to 67 kg/ha] for erosion control; cereal oats, barley, or rye: 60 to 90 lb/acre [67 to 101 kg/ha])

Tilled Annual Legumes

Bell Bean/Fava Bean. Seed this tall-growing (up to 6 ft [1.8 m]) erect vetch annually by November 1 to obtain good growth prior to cold weather. Even though it grows quite tall, it does not produce a lot of biomass. It can fix 100 pounds (45 kg) of nitrogen in low nitrogen soils. (80 to 100 lb/acre [90 to 112 kg/ha])

Lana Vetch. This prolific nitrogen fixer (up to 250 lb/acre [280 kg/ha]) is seeded in the fall and tilled in the spring. The amount of growth depends on seeding date, winter temperatures, rainfall, and tillage date. It grows well in cold weather and is the best choice of cover crop when seeding will be late. (15 to 30 lb/acre [17 to 34 kg/ha])

Common and Purple Vetch. Very similar in growth habits, these two vetches grow well during the winter when seeded in early fall. They will tolerate 20°F (-6.7°C) temperatures without injury. (40 to 50 lb/acre [45 to 56 kg/ha])

Hairy Vetch. This type of vetch is better adapted to sandy soils. It is also very cold tolerant but does not grow much during the winter. (40 to 50 lb/acre [45 to 56 kg/ha])

Field Pea (Austrian or Canadian Winter). This cover crop grows like garden pea, remains almost dormant in cold weather, but growth surges in the spring. (70 to 90 lb/acre [78 to 101 kg/ha])

Fenugreek. Fenugreek germinates in cold conditions as late as December and provides a good stand. (35 to 45 lb/acre [39 to 50 kg/ha])

Combinations. Legumes and grasses are often mixed to produce a dense biomass. Such combinations can be mowed for weed control in the tree row or tilled. One combination that has been used often and successfully in California is oats and vetch. Combinations with several different cover crop species usually end up with one or two dominating the others. This is because of differences in plant height, spread, or vigor due to moisture, temperature, and soil fertility conditions.

3

Disease and Pest Management

Effective management of pathogenic diseases and nonpathogenic disorders is crucial to the success of California's organic apple production. This manual covers in detail the major diseases and disorders affecting apples in California. Minor diseases and disorders are discussed in the context of having different control measures for organic and conventional production systems. In most cases the biology and monitoring of apple pests are identical for organic and conventional production and are well covered in *Integrated Pest Management for Apples and Pears,* 2nd ed. (ANR Publication 3340, 1999). The publication *IPM Guidelines – Apples* (ANR Publication 3339 or see the IPM Web site at http://www. ipm.ucdavis.edu) lists registered pesticides, including some organic alternatives. *Commercial Apple Growing in California* (ANR Publication 2456, 1992) also specifically describes in greater detail many of the common apple diseases, physiological disorders, and problems associated with postharvest handling of fruit.

Because many of the mineral and botanical pest control products used by organic growers are not as effective as synthetic pesticides, timing of application, planning of long-term suppressive measures, and consistent, up-to-date pest monitoring methods are crucial. Costs of organic pest control materials are usually higher and their efficacy is more variable than with most synthetic pesticides. However, the benefits of organic materials may include reductions in future pest resistance, secondary pest outbreaks, regulatory uncertainty, and potential health and environmental effects associated with the more toxic chemical pesticides.

This chapter reviews the principal diseases and physiological disorders along with the organically acceptable control methods that have been tested in California.

MAJOR APPLE DISEASES

Apple Scab

Apple scab is a fungal disease caused by the fungus *Venturia inaequalis.* It thrives in moist and temperate climates and has been a serious problem on the North Coast of California where winters and springs are mild and wet, and summers are often foggy. However, it also occurs in the San Joaquin Valley, Sierra Foothills, Central Coast, and other areas of California when rainy weather continues into late spring. Most commercial varieties, including Golden and Red Delicious, Granny Smith, Gravenstein, Gala, and Fuji, are very susceptible to scab.

If left uncontrolled, apple scab can destroy a crop. Severe infections lead to blossom drop, blemished, misshapen, and dwarfed fruit, and eventually, total fruit drop and defoliated trees (see color plates 3.1 and 3.2). Moderate infection causes reductions in yield and fruit blemishes. Mild infections may not have an immediate effect on the current crop but will maintain high inoculum levels that can result in damage whenever environmental conditions for infection are met.

Symptoms and Life Cycle. Apple scab first appears in early spring as lesions on new leaves, blossoms, and fruit. The small, olive-green lesions are round and scabby on the upper leaf surface, and velvety with an irregular shape on the underside of the leaf. As the lesions grow and spread, infected leaves become twisted and cupped, turn yellow, and fall off. Fruit lesions start out as sooty and black, sometimes surrounded by a red halo, and eventually turn into dry, corky scabs. It takes about 2 to 3 weeks during cool spring weather to find visual symptoms of scab after an infection period.

Badly infected fruit are malformed, undersized, and often drop off the tree prematurely. Fruit are most susceptible from bloom to about 1 week after petal fall. After that, they gradually become more resistant to infections. If conditions are favorable, however, scab infection can also occur close to harvest, causing tiny black to red lesions on the fruit lenticels of mature fruit. This is called *pin point scab*.

The scab fungus overwinters on infected fallen leaves but not in the tree or on twigs or branches. During winter the reproductive structures of the fungus mature in these intact and infected leaves. When scab-infected leaves become wet with rainfall in early spring and temperatures are above 40°F (4.4°C), the leaves emit spores (ascospores) that travel in the wind to new green tissue. The ascospores cause the first (primary) infections. These quickly lead to secondary infections from the asexual spores called conidia and to disease of epidemic proportions.

The scab fungus needs free moisture (rain, heavy dew, or drippy fog) for a specific length of time before it can infect. The required length of the wetness period varies depending on the temperature. Under usual spring and summer temperatures, it only takes 9 to 15 hours of wetness for infection to begin. It is possible that careful monitoring of rainfall and temperatures could reduce the need for some protectant sprays (see Mills Chart in table 3.1). However, in most cases the prediction of weather conditions in the orchard is not exact enough for organic growers to run the risk of skipping a protectant spray.

Control. The key to scab control is to prevent the disease-causing spores from infecting susceptible tissue. This is done by protecting the first green tissues emerging from buds in the spring from primary infections with organic fungicide sprays, by reducing inoculum levels through sanitation methods, or by not

Table 3.1. Mills Chart: Temperature and moisture requirements for scab infections in spring.

| | Hours of wetting required for infection during spring* | | | |
Average temperature (°F)	Light infection	Moderate infection	Heavy infection	Days until lesions appear
33–41	>48	—	—	—
42	30	40	60	—
43	25	34	51	—
44	22	30	45	—
45	20	27	41	—
46	19	25	38	—
47	17	23	35	—
48	15	20	30	17
49	14.5	20	30	17
50	14	19	29	16
51	13	18	27	16
52	12	18	26	15
53	12	17	25	15
54	11.5	16	24	14
55	11	16	24	14
56	11	15	22	13
57	10	14	22	13
58	10	14	21	12
59	10	13	21	12
60	9.5	13	20	11
61	9	13	20	10
62	9	12	19	10
63	9	12	18	9
64	9	12	18	9
65	9	12	18	9
66–75	9	12	18	8
76	9.5	12	19	9
77	11	14	21	9
78	13	17	26	10

* After infection is established and secondary spores are present in large numbers, hours for reinfection are only two-thirds of figures shown.
Source: Statewide Integrated Pest Management Project, University of California Division of Agriculture and Natural Resources.

having susceptible tissue present. A number of alternatives are available to the organic grower to fight scab, including the use of disease-resistant cultivars, preventive cultural practices, and chemical controls. Biological controls, including botanical extracts and antagonistic fungi, are not currently available but are being investigated and may be permitted for use by commercial growers in the near future. The best approach now is to use a combination of all the available control methods. Keep in mind, however, that the organic materials used for apple scab control do not have the preventive residual effect of conventional fungicides and must be applied more frequently. Neither do they have the same aftereffect of some conventional fungicides that can kill newly established infections for up to 120 hours after an infection period, depending on the material used.

Resistant Cultivars. The only certain way for organic growers to control scab year after year is to grow scab-resistant apples. The plant tissue in these varieties is not susceptible to the disease. A number of scab-resistant cultivars are described in chapter 2 of this manual. Before planting new cultivars, growers should determine that there is a viable market for the new varieties. Several newer varieties have excellent culinary characteristics, but no name recognition in the marketplace. There is certainly the potential to grow many of these varieties as processing apples while gleaning the best fruit for the fresh market. Fresh market sales will be more challenging, however, because of the uncertainty of the demand for the variety.

Cultural Controls. Spores that overwinter in leaf litter on the orchard floor cause primary infection in spring. If the overwintering inoculum is reduced or eliminated, the potential incidence of scab is reduced. This will only work, however, in isolated orchards. All of the cultural practices used to limit scab infections will be ineffective where neighboring orchards are full of inoculum that can blow into treated orchards.

The orchard floor can be kept free of leaves by various methods before new bud break in the spring. Fallen leaves can be raked, blown, or vacuumed from beneath trees into the middles and then removed or disked into the soil to decompose before scab ascospores have a chance to mature and develop. Natural decomposition of leaves on the surface of the orchard floor usually does not eliminate ascospore development sufficiently during winter months because of temperature, moisture, and nutrient constraints.

Nitrogen is often the most important missing ingredient limiting the breakdown of apple leaves by microorganisms that cause decomposition. Proper composting of apple leaves at temperatures of 140° to 160°F (60° to 71°C) kills scab spores by eliminating the substrate on which the ascospores develop. The compost may need to be made with additions of manures to aid in leaf breakdown, which can later be used as a fertilizer and soil amendment under trees.

Running a mower over fallen leaves to pulverize them and adding compost or some other source of nitrogen such as blood or feather meals will speed up leaf decomposition directly on the orchard floor. Zinc sulfate can burn the leaves and causes them to fall prematurely. It also has the benefit of providing zinc, an important nutrient for apple trees. This practice has been shown to have no detrimental effect on the following year's growth, bloom, or production. Certifiers may require a defciency report for the application of zinc.

Cover crops were once thought to be barriers to spore release, as well as a source of nutrients to help decompose infected apple leaves. However, no reduction in apple scab incidence has been shown in research orchards with winter cover crops. If the inoculum is there, and spring weather conditions are wet, cover crops do little to stop apple scab spread or infection.

In orchards where overhead irrigation is used, care must be taken to avoid creating conditions ideal for infection. Growers should irrigate only at night, when far fewer ascospores are released. However, once conidia (asexual spores) are present on leaves in the tree, it makes no difference when the wetness occurs (day or night). Irrigation periods should be kept short to prevent infection or spread of the disease. The Mills Chart in table 3.1 can be useful in determining how long it is safe to irrigate at particular air temperatures.

Chemical Controls. Organic chemical control of scab consists of copper, sulfur, and lime-sulfur mixtures (see table 3.2). Under low to moderate disease pressure, these organic fungicides effectively control scab. This is particularly true when they are used early in the disease cycle and when applications are timed correctly. Their primary disadvantage is that in years when disease pressure is high and orchard access is difficult, the organically acceptable materials, which have a shorter residual and less "kick-back" protection, have to be applied more frequently and may not provide adequate control. Kick-back is the eradication of infections that began 24 to 120 hours prior to the application of the fungicide.

Of the organically acceptable products on the market for apple scab control, copper and sulfur minerals are the most effective. They are both much better as protectants and cannot eradicate an infection once it has occurred (kick-back). To be effective, they must be on the plant tissue just prior to and during the infection period. This means that growers must spray when conditions are right for infection, which is just before rain when temperatures are above 40°F (4.4°C) and there is susceptible tissue on the tree.

Fixed copper and micronized sulfurs have been shown to protect against scab as effectively as many of the conventional synthetic fungicides. However, if applied after bloom fixed copper sprays can cause russeting on the fruit even at very low rates (see color plate 3.3). Russeting on apples is a complex disorder caused by several factors, including the variety, weather, humidity, wetness, and spray materials applied. It is very difficult to predict when or how a given management program will cause russeting. Although concentrate sprays usually produce less russeting than dilute sprays, in repeated and large dosages fixed coppers are phytotoxic, toxic to animals, and can persist in the soil.

Copper has a better residual than sulfur and is best applied as the first scab spray of the season prior to bloom, usually at the green tip stage. Rates can reach levels as high as 4 to 8 pounds per acre (4.5 to 9 kg/ha). For processing fruit, where russeting is not a major concern, copper can be used after bloom quite effectively.

Micronized sulfur applied at 10 to 15 pounds per acre (11 to 17 kg/ha) (most materials expressed as 80% sulfur) effectively prevents apple scab infections. It can be applied from green tip through fruit set and fruit development without phytotoxic effects or fruit russeting. The residual for protection is about one week. Therefore, under conditions for scab development sulfur sprays need to be applied weekly.

Sulfur is a mild irritant and gradually acidifies the soil. Sulfur and oil are incompatible and phytotoxic to leaves even when applied separately. They should be applied at least 2 to 3 weeks apart. They should never be tank mixed unless applied to dormant wood. Once leaf development has occurred, care must be taken if oil is used for control of other pests such as aphids or codling moth within 2 to 3 weeks of any sulfur application.

Tank mixes of copper and sulfur together have been tested and evaluated scientifically. When used together, lower rates of each were neither synergistic nor effective, so no particular benefits were observed. However, at full rates, an early application of fixed copper at green tip followed by micronized sulfur after bloom has been effective and does not cause fruit russeting.

Liquid lime sulfur can also be used to prevent apple scab and is the only mineral substance that burns out primary scab infections with repeated applications. It can, however, be phytotoxic and can burn leaves and blossoms if applied during hot weather. Handle liquid lime sulfur with care because it is highly caustic. It is also potentially harmful to mite predators, possibly causing spider mite outbreaks later in the season.

Application rates of up to 12 gallons per acre (112 L/ha) can be applied (3 gal liquid lime sulfur/100 gal water [11L/379L]) from the delayed dormant to the green tip stages alone or mixed with dormant oil. Severe phytotoxicity can occur when high rates of lime sulfur are used or when oil mixtures are applied after green tip. In cool weather, lime sulfur at rates of 1 to 2 gallons per 100 [4L/379L] can be applied at up to 10 percent bloom without leaf burn. Low rates of lime sulfur have been used for many years as a scab control material prior to and after bloom without detrimental effects on fruit set or fruit finish. Care must be taken, however, because applications during or just after bloom have caused blossom and fruit thinning.

Other organic spray materials have been evaluated for scab control on apples. Soaps and oil sprays, while very effective against powdery mildew, reduce scab lesions somewhat but are not nearly as effective as copper and sulfur. These less effective materials might provide adequate control of apple scab where disease inoculum is kept low and when weather con-

Table 3.2. Organic chemical controls for apple scab.

Material	Brand name*	Label rate	Timing	Protective efficacy (days)	Cleanup infection
Fixed coppers	Kocide	4–8 lb/acre	green tip to tight cluster	7–10	none
	COCS	4–8 lb/acre	green tip to tight cluster	7–10	none
	Nu-Cop	4–8 lb/acre	green tip to tight cluster	7–10	none
Micronized sulfurs	Thiolux	10–30 lb/acre	green tip to harvest	5–7	none
	Microthial Special	10–20 lb/acre	green tip to harvest	5–7	none
Calcium polysulfides	lime sulfur solution	2–3 gal/100 acres	green tip to prebloom	5	can burn lesions†
	lime sulfur solution	2–2.5 gal/100 acres	green tip to bloom	5	can burn lesions†
	lime sulfur solution	1 gal/100 acres	green tip to small fruit	5	can burn lesions†

*Brand names are for information only. Check with your certification agency for the current status of any brand-name product.
†Caution should be taken as calcium polysulfides can burn leaves in warm weather.

ditions are less favorable for the disease. Seaweed extracts, fish fertilizers, and compost tea were completely ineffective against apple scab in several trials on the West Coast.

Timing of Chemical Applications. The essential timing for scab control is from green tip through bloom. New tissues produced by rapidly growing trees must be covered with protectant at all times to prevent infection. Copper should be used for at least the first spray at green tip, and perhaps up to tight cluster stage, followed by applications of micronized sulfur. Sulfur lasts only 5 to 10 days and must be applied before or during every primary infection period (rain, dew, and fog) on a weekly basis as long as conditions for infection persist. If there are severe infections that have not become well established, lime sulfur may be used. Two or three applications should burn out the lesions, and then micronized sulfur can be used during the rest of the season. Again, care should be taken not to apply lime sulfur if weather turns hot.

Inoculum levels can also be a factor in determining the need to spray and the specific timing. Sprays can be delayed with dry spring weather in orchards with little or no scab history. Apply treatments only after infection or when rain is forecast. The Mills Chart included in table 3.1 can also help time sprays based on temperature and duration of wetness.

Researchers in the eastern United States have developed a system for predicting potential ascospore dose (PAD) based on a disease and leaf litter assessment and expressed as the number of ascospores per square meter of orchard floor. They have effectively delayed or eliminated early season sprays without detrimental effects. Trials to validate the PAD system have not been conducted in California. It is clear that orchards with a history of disease and frequent spring rains require an aggressive, early, preventive spray program.

In orchards where scab has been kept under control, the grower can wait until tight cluster to start a copper spray. However, if the orchard is near any other apple trees that might provide an external source of inoculum, it might be wise to spray earlier—at green tip—as a precaution. Orchards heavily infested with scab the year before should also receive earlier preventive sprays to reduce the risk of repeated infection.

Biological Controls. Researchers worldwide are investigating the potential of biological organisms and botanical extracts to control scab. Several interesting possibilities include extract of ivy (*Hedera helix*) and fungi antagonistic to scab. Researchers in Switzerland have shown that leaf extracts of ivy inhibited conidia germination under greenhouse conditions. Scientists have also identified at least two species of fungi that attack apple scab. These fungi, *Athelia bombacina* and *Chaetomium globosum,* have been shown to suppress scab ascospore production by up to 100 percent when applied to infected apple leaves under controlled conditions. None of these potential biological controls has been tested under field conditions in California, however, and their availability for commercial use is still unknown.

Flamers. Propane flamers that heat or burn fallen leaves can significantly reduce apple scab primary inoculum (ascospores), leading to reduced disease pressure for several weeks. Research in the eastern and midwestern United States has demonstrated the potential success of this technique, which should also be effective in California. Flaming is expensive, and to be effective the leaves must be heated to very high temperatures, and the ground must be free of any obstructions such as cover crops, prunings, or weeds.

Fire Blight

Fire blight is caused by the bacterium *Erwinia amylovora.* It is classified here as a major disease because periodic epidemics triggered by ideal temperature, humidity, tree growth stage, and varietal interaction can devastate trees. The pathogen overwinters in cankers (dead areas) in bark on the tree and usually attacks blossoms and kills fruiting spurs. It can also infect new succulent shoots and spread rapidly down the tree. Shoots and scaffolds can be lost, and young vigorous trees killed. Apples are far less susceptible than pears, and coastal areas are much less affected than the Central Valley because of temperature differences during bloom.

Symptoms and Disease Cycle. Affected plant parts appear scorched by fire. In the early stages of blossom blight, the flower clusters are wilted as if water-soaked. Infected flowers and leaves remain attached to shoots and turn gray then brown then black as they die. Infection of succulent vegetative shoots often results in a characteristic crook at the tip as they turn black and dry up. A brownish, sticky fluid containing the bacteria often oozes from infected tissue. Cankers are difficult to detect but appear as irregular-shaped, sunken, and dark areas. There are often reddish streaks in the tissue beneath the bark.

Optimum temperatures for growth and spread of fire blight are between 75° and 80°F (23.9° and 26.7°C), but the bacterium will grow at temperatures of 41° to 86°F (5.0° to 30.0°C). As temperatures rise in spring, bacteria begin to multiply at the edges of the previous year's bark cankers. Rain and insects, primarily honey bees, disperse the bacteria to open blossoms and succulent growth. It can quickly become widespread throughout the orchard. If favorable temperatures (above 62°F [16.7°C] in March, 60°F [15.6°C] in April, or 58°F [14.4°C] in May) occur during bloom along with rainfall or very high humidity, control measures will very likely be necessary.

Control. A five-phase approach is useful in controlling fire blight:

1. Reduce inoculum through pruning out infected branches, shoots, and spur cankers as soon as they appear.

2. Moderate growth of tender shoots by limiting water and nitrogen, if possible, especially in early spring.

3. Prevent infections with timely applications of bactericides.

4. Apply biocontrol agents.

5. Grow resistant varieties and rootstocks.

Pruning. Infected spurs and shoots should be removed as soon as they are observed. Pruning cuts should be at least 12 inches (30.5 cm) below the infected tissue. The shears or saw must be cleaned with a disinfectant between cuts because blight bacteria can be spread by the shears or saw if a cut is made through diseased tissue.

Vigor Management. Because organic orchards rely primarily on low concentration, slow-release nitrogen from organic sources such as composts and cover crops, rapid and more succulent shoot growth is naturally avoided. If specific conditions occur to allow irrigation water to be limited until after bloom, vegetative growth can be somewhat controlled and fire blight limited.

Bactericides. Traditionally, fire blight prevention has included one or more blossom applications of certified organic antibiotics (streptomycin sulfate) or fixed copper sprays. Late bloom is particularly susceptible and should be protected; however, sprays have not been shown to prevent shoot infections.

Streptomycin sulfate has a very short residual and should be applied every 3 to 5 days during bloom. However, antibiotic use should be limited in order to avoid and delay bacterial resistance. Treatment requirements should be based on the existence of temperatures, humidity, and rain conditions ideal for fire blight during bloom. Fixed copper sprays are an important tool for controlling fire blight and were used for many years before the development of antibiotic treatments, but fixed copper sprays can also cause severe fruit russeting in some years. When using copper sprays, avoid high rates of copper during the postbloom period in order to reduce the potential for russeting the fruit (see

Chemical Controls in the **Apple Scab** section above). Copper is generally not as effective as antibiotic treatments. It also has a short residual and must be applied every 3 to 7 days to maintain preventive control under conditions favorable to fire blight.

Biocontrol. Fire blight bacteria first become established on the stigma of the flower. Antagonistic (biocontrol) microorganisms occupying the stigma of the flower exclude or resist the fire blight pathogen and prevent infections from becoming established. *Pseudomonas fluorescens,* a bacterium antagonistic to the fire blight pathogen, is currently registered for use as BlightBan A506. It must be present in sufficient numbers and well dispersed to be effective. It is applied every week during bloom to make sure newly opening flowers are colonized by the antagonistic bacterium. A monitoring technique for determining the presence of *Pseudomonas fluorescens* has recently been developed to help determine if additional sprays are needed. There are a number of other potential biocontrol agents that offer promise for future fire blight control, including strains of the bacteria *Erwinia herbicola* and several other bacteria and yeasts.

Resistant Varieties and Rootstocks. Almost all of the currently grown commercial varieties are susceptible to fire blight, though some are more severely affected than others. Part of a variety's susceptibility is related to the quantity of out-of-season or rat-tail bloom, which usually occurs in late spring during warm weather. Varieties with rat-tail bloom should be avoided in fire blight-prone areas. In general, very susceptible varieties include Fuji, Pink Lady, Jonathan, Jonagold, Rome Beauty, and Gala. Somewhat less susceptible varieties include Granny Smith, Red Delicious, Golden Delicious, McIntosh, Stayman Winesap, Williams Pride, and Pristine. These varieties may sustain multiple infections, but they usually do not progress into bigger wood or kill trees.

The commonly used rootstocks M26 and M9 are very susceptible to fire blight and easily killed when infected; seedling rootstock is also very susceptible. These rootstocks should be avoided in areas prone to severe fire blight and not used as understock to very susceptible varieties. M7 is very resistant, and M111 and M106 are somewhat resistant.

MINOR APPLE DISEASES

Powdery Mildew

Powdery mildew is caused by the fungus *Podosphaera leucotricha* and is a common foliage disease of apples in California. A white, powdery growth appears on leaves and shoots. Control can be obtained by removing infected shoots during dormant pruning and new shoots and blossoms as they become infected. Applications of lime sulfur, micronized sulfur, M-pede (soap), or summer oil at pink bud and petal fall stages usually controls this disease, although additional sprays may be needed under some conditions for susceptible varieties. These organic materials have been very effective against powdery mildew, especially in years with low disease pressure. Compost tea, seaweed extracts, and liquid fish fertilizer have not been found to be effective against this disease.

Spray applications for the control of apple scab usually control powdery mildew at the same time. Oil and sulfur sprays should not be applied together or within 2 to 3 weeks of each other because of the potential for leaf burn and fruit russeting.

Phytophthora Root and Crown Rot

The *Phytophthora* species of root and crown rot kills and stunts trees by attacking and destroying primarily trunk and root tissue just below the soil line. Several species of *Phytophthora* are soil-inhabiting fungi requiring the presence of free water (saturated soil conditions) to reproduce and infect the host plant. Therefore, prevention is achieved through the avoidance of saturated soil conditions. This can be accomplished by providing good surface drainage away from low areas before planting and installing subsurface drainage. Drip emitters should be placed 18 to 24 inches (45.7 to 61 cm) away from tree trunks to avoid constant moisture near the trunks. Planting trees on ridges or mounds can dramatically help reduce crown rot. In addition, weeds should not be allowed to grow around the crown because they maintain high humidity. Cover crops in row middles eliminate excessive soil moisture more than clean cultivated ground. In some other tree species, heavy organic mulches have been shown to reduce the incidence of *Phytophthora* rots. In those trials, 3 to 4 inches (7.5 to 10 cm) of fresh wood chips were placed around the base of trees for weed control but simultaneously reduced the incidence of root rot. All apple rootstocks currently in use are susceptible. However, M111 shows some resistance to common *Phytophthora* species in the Central Valley, while M106 shows some resistance to the *Phytophthora* species more common in coastal areas.

Oak Root Fungus

Caused by the soil-inhabiting fungus *Armellaria melia*, oak root fungus spreads slowly in a circular pattern from tree to tree through root grafts and soil movement. Apples have some resistance to this disease, but

will succumb if inoculum is high or the strain is particularly virulent.

Prevention from the start of orchard planning is the key to managing oak root fungus, which is almost impossible to control in an existing organic planting. Start with a site that did not previously have woodland trees or a previous orchard. If an old orchard is being removed, take extra time to remove all the old roots possible. For an existing orchard, remove the diseased tree(s) and all healthy adjacent trees, as well; infection of the latter may have already begun. Dig up and burn all remaining roots greater than 1 inch (2.5 cm) in diameter on infected and adjacent trees; do not allow infected roots to spread to uninfested areas. Solarization, heavy applications of compost, or use of *Trichoderma* (beneficial fungi) will not prevent, eradicate, or control oak root fungus, but should help replants get off to a good start and may delay infection.

Dematophora Root Rot

The fungus *Roselinia necatrix* causes Dematophora root rot, primarily in the Central Coast area. It is a root rotting disease that causes yellowing of foliage and poor branch growth, while below ground, the fibrous roots are rotted. There are no satisfactory control methods once the tree has the disease. Prevention by avoiding soils where it has previously been present is the key to control.

Sappy Bark

Sappy bark is a condition caused by the fungus *Trametes versicolor*. It is common in many growing districts, especially on old trees. The fungus spreads in wet, windy weather and infects pruning wounds and sunburned areas. The disease spreads slowly within the tissue, moving a few inches each year. Dead limbs have soft bark that is spongy in wet weather and peels off in paper-thin pieces in dry weather. Control is achieved by removing diseased limbs below the infected area, preventing sunburning of limbs, and avoiding large pruning cuts that provide infection points. Avoid pruning during wet weather and make clean cuts that are less likely to become infected. Treating large pruning wounds with Bordeaux paste or a strong detergent has shown some preventive potential.

Southern Blight

The fungus *Sclerotium rolfsii* causes southern blight disease. It has killed young trees (under 4 years old) in Southern California, but has not yet appeared in the northern part of the state. Older infected trees can sometimes overcome the disease and recover. Infected trees often have a web of white mycelium on the soil at the tree base. The fungus girdles the trunk and rapidly kills the tree, usually leaving brown leaves attached. Later fungal fruiting bodies called sclerotia are present and appear as hard, round spore structures that are initially whitish, then gradually become reddish-brown at maturity. Sclerotia persist in the soil for several years, especially in soils containing a large quantity of organic matter.

Avoid planting in soils containing five or more sclerotia per kilogram of soil. Sclerotia usually come from previously infected crops such as tomatoes, carrots, potatoes, lettuce, alfalfa, clovers, or beans. Soil removal and replacement with clean soil in the planting hole will prevent infection of newly planted trees because the sclerotia must be within 1.25 inches (3.18 cm) of the trunk to cause infection. Some control can be achieved by deep plowing and allowing the field to go fallow for at least 1 year before planting. Southern blight grows profusely in humid conditions, so weed control next to tree trunks also helps by reducing humidity.

European Canker

Frequent outbreaks of this disease, caused by the fungi *Nectria galligena*, have occurred in coastal orchards. Infections occur through leaf scars during autumn rains. Cankers later develop and slowly girdle and kill the branch. Existing cankers should be pruned out. Infection can be prevented if a fixed copper fungicide is applied before autumn rains begin and during early leaf fall, usually in late October.

Postharvest Rots

There are several disease organisms that attack apple fruits after harvest and during storage. The more common are *Alternaria, Stemphillium, Penicillium, Phomopsis, Botrytis, Mucor piriformis,* and *Pezicula malicorticis.* Most cause the fruit flesh to turn soft and brown. Careful handling during harvest, transit, storage, and packing can control these diseases. Bruises, cuts, or punctures provide entry for most of these organisms. Cold temperature storage (33°F [0.6°C]) reduces the likelihood of infection and spread. Care should be taken to thoroughly clean the dump tank at the beginning and end of the season to prevent the introduction of fruit contaminants. Direct sunlight exposure of empty bins for 30 minutes will kill *Mucor piriformis* if present on the wood or plastic.

In recent research, several biocontrol agents have been shown to reduce many of the postharvest rotting organisms such as *Botrytis cinerea, Penicillium expansum,* and *Mucor piriformis.* Two new organically acceptable products, Bio-Save 1000 and Aspire, work by covering the fruit with a beneficial organism that competes with harmful pathogens for nutrients and space at the sites of wounds in fruits.

Viruses

Several viruses have affected apples and their rootstocks, primarily from uncertified (unclean) budwood sources. Virus symptoms include mosaic-patterned chlorotic leaves, distorted branches, irregular markings in the fruit color, necrotic line at the graft union, and deformed fruit with wart-like swellings. Virus-infected rootstocks are less vigorous and dwarf the scion portion of the tree.

Since most viruses are transmitted through propagation wood, control is achieved in most cases by selecting certified virus-free trees and rootstocks from a reputable nursery and avoiding grafting or budwood from infected trees. Once a virus is present, the only control is to remove the tree. Most viruses will not spread from tree to tree, with the exception of the apple union necrosis virus, which is transmitted by the dagger nematode (*Xiphinema americanum*).

....

MAJOR PHYSIOLOGICAL DISORDERS

Bitter Pit

Bitter pit is a common physiological disorder that usually appears just before harvest or during early storage. It is essentially a calcium deficiency of the fruit that is encouraged by excessive tree vigor, over fertilization with nitrogen, extreme fluctuation in soil moisture, light crops, large fruit, or unfavorable soil chemistry. Harvesting immature fruit, cooling delays after harvest, and prolonged storage periods also aggravate this disorder. Mutsu, Golden Delicious, Yellow Newtown, Jonathan, Red Delicious, and Granny Smith are especially susceptible, although any young, rapidly growing variety may exhibit symptoms.

Symptoms. Dark, sunken spots (¼ to ⅜ in [6.5 to 9.5 mm] in diameter) appear on the fruit, especially near the calyx (see color plate 3.4). Bitter pit is sometimes seen on trees just before harvest but more frequently appears after a period of cold storage.

Control. There are eight procedures that will help reduce or eliminate bitter pit:

1. Correct soil pH.

2. Add calcium to soil.

3. Reduce excess vigor.

4. Set a moderate to heavy crop load.

5. Maintain good water management.

6. Apply foliar calcium sprays.

7. Use a postharvest calcium fruit dip.

8. Conduct rapid postharvest fruit cooling.

Most California soils have adequate calcium for apple production. However, a soil pH below 6.0 can reduce calcium availability and should be adjusted by adding a liming material to bring the pH up to between 6.0 and 6.5. Do not use dolomite lime as its high magnesium content can also interfere with calcium uptake. If the soil has an exchangeable calcium to magnesium ratio of less than 5:1, it may be advisable to add a low magnesium-high calcium lime product. Gypsum (calcium sulfate) does not affect pH and can be used to increase the available calcium when a pH adjustment is not needed.

Calcium movement in apples occurs with the movement of water in the trees, so adequate calcium is better provided in trees that are never water stressed. Irrigate frequently (daily) with drip irrigation systems and periodically with surface or sprinkler irrigation to maintain a steady moisture (and calcium) supply to the trees.

Adjust growing practices to reduce excessive vigor and encourage a normal to heavy fruit set in susceptible varieties. Be prudent with leguminous cover crops, manures, and other fertilizers. Too much nitrogen can lead to rank growth, and too much potassium can interfere with calcium uptake. Provide proper conditions for a good fruit set (bees and pollenizer varieties) and careful thinning, if needed, to regulate the crop load. Too light a crop set or over thinning encourages larger fruit and more bitter pit. Do not prune trees heavily in the dormant season as this can encourage excessive vegetative growth. Pruning in the delayed dormant stage or in summer may help to reduce excessive vigor.

When these practices do not provide sufficient control, it may be necessary to apply foliar sprays of calcium during the growing season. There are now several organically acceptable forms of calcium on the market, but not all calcium-containing compounds are effective or acceptable under state and federal organic standards. Those that have been successfully tested are Calcium 25, Stoma Feast, and This Calcium. Consult your certifier about the current acceptability of these products.

Depending on the variety, at least three applications of calcium are usually made (in mid-June, mid-July, and mid-August). Applications may be made at 30-day intervals if using dilute solutions (300 to 400 gal/acre [2808 to 3744 L/ha]) and handgun sprayers. Up to eight applications may be necessary with low-volume (100 to 200 gal/acre [936 to 1872 L/ha]) speed sprayer applications, particularly if bitter pit is severe. In most cases, calcium can be added to the tank mix when applying other sprays, but check the label for compatibility.

If the disorder appears in storage rather than in the field, a postharvest calcium dip may be substituted for the orchard sprays. A 60-second dip into a 2 percent calcium chloride solution (Calcium 25) has been shown to be effective in reducing bitter pit in storage.

Rapid cooling of harvested fruit before packing is critical in reducing bitter pit. A delay of even 24 hours before fruit is properly cooled can increase the incidence of bitter pit in storage by 25 percent or more.

....

MINOR PHYSIOLOGICAL DISORDERS

Water Core

Water core is a physiological disorder that appears as a water-soaked area in and around the core. It is more prevalent under intense heat and sunlight conditions, especially near harvest. The most susceptible varieties are Red Delicious, Granny Smith, and to a lesser extent, Fuji. Harvesting fruit before water core develops attains control.

Apple Measles (Internal Bark Necrosis)

This disorder is caused by magnesium toxicity in acidic soils. It appears as reddish brown pustules on the bark of young branches and stunts tree growth. It is controlled through lime applications that raise soil pH above 6.0.

··

INSECT AND MITE MANAGEMENT

Codling Moth

Codling moth (*Cydia pomonella*) is probably the most serious insect pest that organic apple growers encounter. It occurs in all apple-growing regions of California and has the potential to damage the entire crop if not actively controlled. This is a difficult pest to control organically and requires a thorough understanding of the codling moth life cycle, careful observation throughout the season, and a combination of control approaches.

Life Cycle and Damage. Codling moth overwinters in the orchard under loose bark, in branch crotches, pruning stubs, orchard floor debris, bins and field boxes, wood piles, and the soil around the base of the tree. It overwinters as mature larvae inside a silken cocoon, pupates in early spring, and emerges as an adult a short time later.

The adult is a small, mottled, gray-brown moth, about ½ inch (12.5 mm) in length with a distinctive broad, coppery band at the tip of the wings (see color plate 3.5). They mate and lay eggs in the few hours just before and after sunset when the temperature is 62°F (16.7°C) or greater.

Eggs are laid singly on smooth leaf surfaces or on fruit. Newly laid eggs are clear, flat disks about the size of a pinhead. As eggs mature they turn an opaque white and develop an orange-red ring around the edge. The black head of the larva becomes visible inside the egg during the last few days before hatching (see color plate 3.6).

Larvae are pinkish white with a black to mottled brown head and vary in length from about ⅕ inch (5 mm) at hatching to ¾ inch (19 mm) when mature. They seek out and enter an apple within 24 hours of hatching. As the larvae burrow toward the center of the fruit, reddish-brown frass builds up at the entry site. This frass is very characteristic of codling moth

and the most obvious sign of an infestation. When the larval stage is complete, mature larvae leave the fruit, find suitable pupation sites, and later emerge as adult moths to begin a new generation of mating, egg laying, larval feeding, and pupation. Mating of adults is facilitated by female-emitted pheromones or sex odors that are used by the male to locate females in the orchard.

The number of generations that occur each season and the time it takes to complete each generation depend on the growing region's climate. In the cooler, coastal regions there are typically two generations each year. In the hot northern San Joaquin Valley there are usually three generations each year. And in the very hot southern San Joaquin Valley there may be as many as four generations. Because damage is greater in areas with more generations per year, the areas with fewer generations are preferable for growing organic apples. Table 3.3 shows the variation in codling moth flight activity among various growing regions.

Wormy apples cannot be sold on the fresh market and the damage left by the codling moth makes the apple susceptible to rot and toxin-producing fungal organisms, which greatly limit the saleability of the fruit for juice and other cull uses.

Monitoring. It is important to establish a regular monitoring program to determine when the codling moth is active and the severity of the population (or pressure) in order to take the most appropriate and effective control measures. Traps, degree-day calculation, and careful, regular orchard scouting should all be used to develop the most effective monitoring and control program.

Traps and Lures. Traps baited with pheromone lures are the most commonly used monitoring tool. Pheromone lures mimic the chemical signal that female codling moths emit to attract a mate. Male moths are attracted to the trap in search of a mate. The primary purpose of the traps is to indicate when each generation begins (the biofix) so that treatments can be more accurately timed. Trap catches can also be a valuable

Table 3.3. Average dates for the beginning of each codling moth flight in four California apple growing regions.

Flight	Central Coast (Watsonville)	North Coast (Sebastopol)	Northern San Joaquin Valley (Brentwood)	Southern San Joaquin Valley (Bakersfield)
Overwintering generation (1st flight)	early April	early April	late March	mid-March
1st generation (2d flight)	late June	mid–late June	mid-June	early June
2d generation (3d flight)	late August–early September*	mid-August	early August	mid-July
3d generation (4th flight)	none	none	none	mid-August

*A 3d flight occurs only some years.
Source: Integrated Pest Management for Apples and Pears, 2nd ed. (ANR Publication 3340, 1999), p. 82.

indication of the relative year-to-year timing and intensity of codling moth flight pressure in a specific orchard. Codling moth flight patterns and accumulated seasonal moths are an extremely important yearly reference point for a specific orchard, although they are often not indicative of damage potential, and inter-orchard comparison is often confounded by environmental factors and management programs.

When using pheromone traps, it is important to follow the same procedures each year so the trapping data can be accurately interpreted and compared. Traps should be placed in each orchard for which pest projections are to be made and positioned in the same general area before codling moth flight begins each year.

There are a variety of trap types and lures currently on the market. Follow the manufacturers' directions for assembling and servicing the traps and changing the lures. Lures need to be replaced every 3 to 8 weeks, depending on the brand. Make sure to remove old lures from the trap to prevent them from interfering with the attractiveness of the new lure. It is also a good idea to open the lure package and let it air out for a day or two before installation to avoid an artificial increase in trap activity caused by the fresh lure. Before use, store closed lure packages in the refrigerator or freezer to maintain potency.

Traps baited with lures should be hung on the north side of the tree about 6 to 7 feet (1.8 to 2.1 m) high and at least 100 feet (30.5 m) in from the edge of the orchard. There should be one trap every 10 acres (4 ha) and at least two traps per orchard. Don't place traps closer together than 300 feet (91.4 m) as they may interfere with each other. If the orchard history indicates hot spots where codling moths are more active, make sure to place traps in those locations.

Traps should be put out at bloom, or just before the expected adult moth emergence in spring (see table

3.3). *Biofix* is the date that marks the beginning of each generation; degree-day accumulation begins from that point. In spring, the biofix is the first date that moths are consistently found in traps *and* sunset temperatures are at least 62°F (16.7°C). For later generations, the biofix is determined by an increase in trap catches around the time a new generation should begin.

Traps should be checked twice a week until the biofix is established and can be checked once a week thereafter. When checking traps, count and record the number of codling moths trapped each week, and then clean the trap bottom of insects and debris. Stir the stickum on the trap bottom to keep it sticky. Change the trap bottom monthly or more frequently if it gets too dirty to catch moths. The total number of moths caught per season can also provide relative information about the codling moth pressure in the orchard. When evaluating these counts graphically, often the peaks of codling moth capture are not discrete and may appear as two or more distinct peaks, especially after the previous generation has experienced cool temperatures unsuitable for mating or emergence. Therefore, it is important to compare catch patterns to information provided by degree-day summing (see below).

Degree-Days. Degree-days (°D) are used in conjunction with the pheromone trap information to predict insect development and treatment timing. Degree-days are calculations that combine both temperature and time factors to predict how rapidly the insect will develop under a particular climatic regime. For codling moth, developmental thresholds of 50°F (10°C) and 88°F (31.1°C) are typically used (see table 3.4). Codling moth does not proceed with its development until orchard temperatures are within this range.

Temperature information for calculating degree-days should be gathered from a recording device in the orchard. A maximum-minimum thermometer, recording thermograph, or computerized weather station may be used. The instrument should be housed in an official weather shelter out of direct sunlight and with adequate ventilation. The shelter should be placed about 5 feet (1.5 m) from the ground and away from buildings, roadways, sprinklers, or other anomalies that might influence temperatures. Temperatures from a nearby weather station (CIMIS or NOAA) that is representative of the orchard may also be used if data from the orchard are unavailable.

Degree-day calculations can be made by hand using a degree-day table (see table 3.5) or by computer. The website (http://www.ipm.ucdavis.edu) for the University of California's Integrated Pest Management Project provides access to a wide network of weather stations and a degree-day calculator for use with their data or your own.

Table 3.4. Temperature thresholds and degree-day requirements for codling moth development based on a lower threshold of 50°F (10°C) and an upper threshold of 88°F (31°C).

Event	Degree-days (°D) required	Average degree-days (°D)
Preoviposition period	30–79	58
Egg hatch begins	111–214	158
Larval development	330–640	471
Pupal development	302–586	431
Generation time*	743–1,440	1,060†

*Generation time is the average total time, in degree-days, from initial adult egg laying to the emergence of adults and the initial laying of new eggs in the subsequent generation.

†Generation time for summer flights averages an additional 160°D.

Source: *Integrated Pest Management for Apples and Pears,* 2nd ed. (ANR Publication 3340, 1999), p. 80.

Control. Selecting an orchard or site that has low codling moth pressure, is isolated from nearby sources of infestation, and has early maturing varieties is the best preparation an organic orchardist can make to limit damage from this pest. Once the orchard is selected and planted, seasonal codling moth control will depend on a combination of cultural, biological, and organically acceptable chemical approaches.

Mating Disruption. Mating disruption is the most promising codling moth control option available for organic growers and currently forms the foundation for most successful organic control programs. With this technique, dispensers containing high doses of mating pheromone are hung throughout the orchard. The orchard becomes saturated with the synthetic pheromone which overloads the senses of the male moth, interferes with his ability to find a mate, and disrupts the reproductive cycle.

Orchard sites. Not all orchards are equally suited to the mating disruption technique. Success with mating disruption pheromone depends on the size, shape, and terrain of the orchard, as well as the codling moth pressure.

Orchards should be at least 5 acres (2 ha) in size to provide enough canopy volume to retain an effective dose of the pheromone in the fruit production area of the canopy. A square shape minimizes the area along the edge of the orchard. The edges are more vulnerable to failure because wind moves the pheromone out of

Table 3.5. Degree-day table for codling moth based on a lower threshold of 50°F and an upper threshold of 88°F.*

Max	Minimum temperatures																											
temps	90	88	86	84	82	80	78	76	74	72	70	68	66	64	62	60	58	56	54	52	50	48	46	44	42	40	38	36
118	38	38	38	37	37	36	36	35	35	34	33	32	32	31	30	29	28	28	27	26	25	24	24	23	23	22	22	21
116	38	38	38	37	37	36	36	35	34	34	33	32	31	31	30	29	28	27	27	26	25	24	24	23	23	22	22	21
114	38	38	38	37	37	36	36	35	34	34	33	32	31	31	30	29	28	27	26	26	25	24	23	23	22	22	21	21
112	38	38	38	37	37	36	36	35	34	34	33	32	31	30	30	29	28	27	26	25	24	24	23	22	22	22	21	21
110	38	38	38	37	37	36	36	35	34	33	33	32	31	30	29	28	28	27	26	25	24	23	23	22	22	21	21	20
108	38	38	38	37	37	36	35	35	34	33	32	32	31	30	29	28	27	27	26	25	24	23	22	22	21	21	20	20
106	38	38	38	37	37	36	35	35	34	33	32	31	31	30	29	28	27	26	25	24	24	23	22	22	21	21	20	20
104	38	38	38	37	37	36	35	34	34	33	32	31	30	30	29	28	27	26	25	24	23	22	22	21	21	20	20	19
102	38	38	38	37	37	36	35	34	34	33	32	31	30	29	28	27	27	26	25	24	23	22	21	21	20	20	19	19
100	38	38	38	37	36	36	35	34	33	32	32	31	30	29	28	27	26	25	24	23	22	22	21	20	20	19	19	19
98	38	38	38	37	36	36	35	34	33	32	31	30	30	29	28	27	26	25	24	23	22	21	21	20	19	19	19	18
96	38	38	38	37	36	35	35	34	33	32	31	30	29	28	27	26	25	24	23	23	22	21	20	20	19	19	18	18
94	38	38	38	37	36	35	34	33	33	32	31	30	29	28	27	26	25	24	23	22	21	20	20	19	18	18	18	17
92	38	38	37	37	36	35	34	33	32	31	30	29	28	27	26	25	24	23	22	21	20	20	19	18	18	17	17	17
90	38	38	37	36	36	35	34	33	32	31	30	29	28	27	26	25	24	23	22	21	20	19	18	18	17	17	16	16
88		38	37	36	35	34	33	32	31	30	29	28	27	26	25	24	23	22	21	20	19	18	18	17	16	16	16	15
86			36	35	34	33	32	31	30	29	28	27	26	25	24	23	22	21	20	19	18	17	17	16	15	15	15	14
84				34	33	32	31	30	29	28	27	26	25	24	23	22	21	20	19	18	17	16	16	15	15	14	14	13
82					32	31	30	29	28	27	26	25	24	23	22	21	20	19	18	17	16	15	15	14	14	13	13	12
80						30	29	28	27	26	25	24	23	22	21	20	19	18	17	16	15	14	14	13	13	12	12	11
78							28	27	26	25	24	23	22	21	20	19	18	17	16	15	14	13	13	12	12	11	11	11
76								26	25	24	23	22	21	20	19	18	17	16	15	14	13	12	12	11	11	10	10	10
74									24	23	22	21	20	19	18	17	16	15	14	13	12	11	11	10	10	9	9	9
72										22	21	20	19	18	17	16	15	14	13	12	11	10	10	9	9	8	8	8
70											20	19	18	17	16	15	14	13	12	11	10	9	9	8	8	8	7	7
68												18	17	16	15	14	13	12	11	10	9	8	8	7	7	7	6	6
66													16	15	14	13	12	11	10	9	8	7	7	6	6	6	6	5
64														14	13	12	11	10	9	8	7	6	6	5	5	5	5	4
62															12	11	10	9	8	7	6	5	5	5	4	4	4	4
60																10	9	8	7	6	5	4	4	4	3	3	3	3
58																	8	7	6	5	4	3	3	3	3	2	2	2
56																		6	5	4	3	2	2	2	2	2	2	1
54																			4	3	2	2	1	1	1	1	1	1
52																				2	1	1	1	0	0	0	0	0
50																					0	0	0	0	0	0	0	0
48																						0	0	0	0	0	0	0

* To find total degree-days for a day, locate the low and high temperatures and follow the column and row to where they intersect. For odd-numbered temperatures, interpolate between numbers.

Source: Statewide Integrated Pest Management Project, University of California Division of Agriculture and Natural Resources

the border trees and mated moths fly in from adjacent areas. Compact and continuous canopies without significant gaps also help reduce air movement and retain an even distribution and uniform concentration of synthetic pheromone within the canopy. Hilly terrain may reduce effectiveness because the pheromone is heavier than air and sinks into low areas, leaving high areas unprotected.

Codling moth pressure in surrounding areas is also important. When populations in surrounding areas are high, random matings are more likely, and already mated females are more apt to fly in and lay eggs in the pheromone-treated orchard. For this reason, it can be very difficult to "clean up" an organic orchard that has a poor codling moth management history or is subject to high pressure from surrounding areas.

In cool climates, isolated orchards, and other low pressure sites, mating disruption has been effective as a single tactic approach. In warm interior valleys and other high pressure areas, mating disruption may need to be combined with other organic treatments to obtain satisfactory control. It is important to remember that mating disruption technology is selective for codling moth, so only codling moth mating is affected. All other potential pest problems must be closely monitored.

Products. Several codling moth mating disruption products are currently registered in California, and other products are being developed. Each product has a different field longevity (from 60 to 120 days) and application rate (from 100 to 400 dispensers per acre [112 to 448 dispensers/ha]), so the manufacturer's recommendation for reapplication timing and rate should be carefully followed. Current material costs range from $75 to $110 per application per acre (0.4 ha), and two to three applications are required per season depending on product and climate. The application time can vary from 1 to 2 acres (0.4 to 0.8 ha) per person per hour depending on the product, the application rate, and the size of the canopy.

Regardless of which product is used, the first application should always be made in spring just before the adult codling moths are expected to emerge. This allows pheromone levels to build before moths begin to fly and mate. The dispensers should be placed in the upper third of the canopy. A higher placement may allow too much pheromone to be blown away, and a lower placement leaves the tree tops unprotected. In high density orchards where trees are planted on dwarfing rootstock, pheromones can be placed in the tree by hand, whereas in standard orchards, application poles may be needed.

The full label rate should be used in organic orchards even in low pressure sites, as there is a risk of sustaining damage in vulnerable areas of any orchard. An undetected population may develop to high levels, which can be difficult to bring under control by organic means. Dispensers may be concentrated in problem spots (edges, high spots, narrow areas) to decrease the likelihood of damage. If there is a delay in application or reapplication of the pheromone, mating and egg laying may occur and a supplemental control may be needed to prevent damage.

Monitoring. Careful monitoring is extremely important for the success of a mating disruption program to assure that the system has not broken down, allowing unchecked mating to occur. The best monitoring method is to walk the orchard and look for eggs or fruit damage at least once each potential codling moth generation. Eggs may be difficult to find but are easier to spot early in the season when there is less foliage and apples are small. Larval damage is more obvious and will be visible several weeks after egg laying has occurred (several weeks after initial trap catches).

Scouting can be quite time-consuming, and many growers use pheromone traps to assist with the monitoring. Traps should be hung at the same level as the pheromone dispensers. Both standard 1 mg and supercharged 10 mg lures can be used. They should be placed in all vulnerable areas in the orchard and checked weekly. Traps with 1 mg lures are used to verify that mating is being disrupted; if the pheromone dispensers are working, these traps should not catch any moths. If the traps do catch moths, it is a good indication that egg-laying has occurred. The supercharged traps are helpful in monitoring moth flights and establishing biofix dates that will help in decision making for reapplication. These traps are easier for the moths to find than traps with 1 mg lures and may catch a few moths in a week without indicating the likelihood of mating or fruit damage (see color plate 3.7). Safe numbers of moths caught in traps have not been determined, so any catch should always be followed by a careful examination of fruit in the area surrounding the trap. If eggs or damage are detected, a supplemental control (organic spray, parasitoid wasp release, fruit removal) should be employed, and the pheromone may need to be reapplied. It is also entirely possible to sustain fruit damage without catching any moths in pheromone traps, so periodic fruit monitoring is recommended even if no moths are found in the traps.

Organically Acceptable Spray Materials. Several organic sprays are registered or about to be registered for codling moth control. They appear to be most useful as a control in low pressure settings such as cool coastal orchards or as a supplement to orchards on a mating disruption program.

Codling moth granulosis virus (CMGV). This is a microbial insecticide that has shown promise, although it has had rather mixed success. This may be due to differences in application volume, adjuvants, product handling, and perhaps even product viability. It has proved most effective when applied at higher volumes (200 gal/acre [1872 L/ha]) with NuFilm-17 at a pH of 6. The CMGV must be eaten by the larvae to be effective. Therefore, it has to be on the fruit as the larvae hatch since they only feed for a short time on the surface before entering the fruit (where they are protected from sprays). CMGV degrades quickly with light and heat and must be reapplied at weekly intervals during hatchout. This could lead to as many as 18 to 20 sprays over the course of the season in hot interior climates but as few as 6 sprays in cooler coastal areas with less pressure. If used as a supplement to mating disruption in high pressure sites, the peak hatchout period can be targeted and fewer sprays used. Codling moths infected with CMGV may live long enough to sting or penetrate fruit but not long enough to do serious damage. CMGV is not currently available, but California registration of a formulation (Carpovirusine) is expected.

Summer oil. This substance can be effective in low pressure situations but is only mildly effective under high codling moth pressure. It works by smothering eggs and needs to be applied frequently during egg laying periods. Its use is limited, as there is a danger of phytotoxicity if applied during hot summer weather. Summer oil cannot be used within a few weeks of a sulfur application, limiting its use during rainy springs when sulfur is applied for scab control. Good coverage is essential. A 1 to 2 percent solution applied at a rate of 100 to 200 gallons of solution per acre (936 to 1872 L/ha) has been effective. Use the 1 percent solution if temperatures are expected to approach 90°F (32.2°C).

Other methods. Bt (*Bacillus thuringiensis*), rotenone, and pyrethrum are other organic materials that are registered for use on apples; however, these materials have not proved effective against codling moth in field trials. It has been suggested that thinning fruit to one per cluster may improve the efficacy of these low-toxicity spray materials by allowing for more complete fruit coverage. Nevertheless, recent research has not shown this to be the case.

Biological Control. Because codling moth is not a native pest to California, the native beneficial insects are not very effective in controlling it. There are a number of generalist predators that eat codling moth but are not at all specialized for this pest and are not able to keep the populations below economically acceptable levels on their own. These predators include ground beetles, ants, spiders, earwigs, and lacewings. Birds and small mammals have also been reported to consume codling moth. Since they can provide some supplemental control at little cost to the grower, it might be prudent to encourage these predators by assuring they have suitable habitat in orchards.

There are also five naturally occurring parasitoids in California that attack codling moth. *Trichogramma platneri* is a parasitoid of codling moth eggs. *Ascogaster quadridentatus* is an egg-larval parasitoid attacking the egg stage but killing the codling moth larva only after it has completed feeding and spun a cocoon under the bark or on the ground. *Macrocentrus ancylivorus* is a larval parasitoid. *Dibrachys cavus* and in coastal regions *Mastrus carpocapsae* attack cocooned larvae. None of these parasitoids has a great impact on the codling moth populations in their natural settings. However, the native wasp *Trichogramma platneri* has significantly reduced codling moth populations when regular releases of commercially raised wasps have been conducted throughout the season.

The *Trichogramma platneri* wasp pupae are currently available on cardboard tabs from commercial insectaries. The tabs can be hung, stapled, taped, or otherwise affixed to shaded outer leaves and branches on the north side of the tree. If placed close to the tree trunk, they are more susceptible to damage from ants, earwigs, and other predators. If this type of predation becomes a problem, the tabs can be enclosed in small paper cups perforated with a few pin holes or in small, mesh-wire screen cages that are then hung in the orchard. In orchards where trees are planted with standard spacing, every tree should be treated; in high density orchards, releases should be made every 20 to 30 feet (6 to 9 m) in each row. The cups or tabs should be hung in a regular pattern to encourage an even dispersal throughout the orchard.

In apples, inundative releases have been most effective in low pressure sites and in conjunction with a mating disruption program. Releases of 100,000 wasps per acre (30 tabs) each week during active egg-laying periods (peak flight periods) have been successful. Releases can be made throughout the entire orchard. If codling moth pressure is very low and there is a negligible resident population, releases can be restricted to the areas that are vulnerable in a mating disruption program (edges, high spots, areas near adjacent orchards).

There are several, more specialized codling moth parasites that have recently been imported from Central Asia, where codling moth is native. Their adaptability to California conditions and their effect on local codling moth populations are being studied. Recent observations indicate that *Mastrus ridibuadus,* a gregarious parasitoid of cocooned larvae, has become established in California, but it is too soon to know what impact it will have on codling moth populations.

Cultural Controls. One of the most important aspects of organic control is eliminating potential reservoirs of infestation from within and around the orchard. Good sanitation practices should include the removal of cull piles, bins, props, and other debris that could provide overwintering sites for codling moth.

Some varieties of apple drop codling moth–damaged fruit. While removal of this dropped fruit has been a standard sanitation recommendation for organic orchards, recent research has shown that only a small percentage of the fallen fruit actually contain larvae. The larvae leave the fruit within a day or two of falling. Therefore, the expense of daily removal of dropped fruit should be weighed against the limited benefit of this practice. This technique has been most effective for Gravensteins and Golden Delicious.

A more effective sanitation practice is to remove codling moth–infested fruit from the tree before it is damaged enough to drop and the larvae have had a chance to move on. Infested fruit should be removed from the orchard or destroyed to prevent larvae from crawling out and reinfesting the orchard. A single, well-timed effort at each generation may be quite worthwhile in reducing populations, especially in short, high density orchards. Fruit removal should be completed by the time 630 degree-days have accumulated in each generation, as this is the earliest that mature larvae are likely to leave the fruit. This approach has been successfully used as a supplement to mating disruption in vulnerable areas where damage has occurred.

Physical controls. Placing special fruit bags over young fruit at thinning time is a technique that has been used in Japan to control a number of pests. Research in California has shown this to be an effective technique in controlling sunburn, codling moth, and other pests, as well as improving fruit color in red varieties. However, the high cost ($3,000 to $10,000/acre) and high time requirement limit this approach for large-scale operations.

Other techniques, such as placing cardboard bands around trunks to trap pupating larvae and scraping loose bark from older trees to reduce the number of pupation sites, have been suggested as organic controls. These approaches are not practical on a commercial scale, and their effectiveness in reducing populations is questionable. In fact, if trunk bands are not removed and destroyed in a timely fashion, they could actually aid in increasing the codling moth population.

OTHER ARTHROPOD PESTS

Most other occasional pests in organic apple orchards (aphids, mites, scale, leafrollers) can be controlled with organically acceptable materials. Properly applied dormant (when buds are dormant in January and February) and delayed dormant (at green tip in March) oil sprays are fundamental in the control of these pests. Dormant oil formulations should be examined in close consultation with certifers' brand name lists to select allowable materials. Follow the manufacturer's directions for dormant and delayed dormant applications. Leafrollers can also be controlled with in-season applications of *Bacillus thuringiensis* (Bt) formulations. Without disruption of biological control by early season insecticide applications, leafminers, mites, and most aphids are controlled by native predacious and parasite insects and are only occasionally a problem in consistently well-managed organic apple orchards. Portions of the aphid and mite descriptions are adapted from *Commercial Apple Growing in California* (ANR Publication 2456, 1992).

Aphids

There are three aphids found on apples in California: rosy apple aphid, woolly apple aphid, and green apple aphid. The type and amount of damage caused varies depending on the aphid species present.

In organic orchards, natural enemies frequently keep aphid populations below damaging levels. The important predators that attack aphids in apples include several species of lady beetles, green and brown lacewings, soldier beetles, and syrphid fly larvae. Some aphid species, in particular the woolly apple aphid, are also attacked by parasitic wasps.

Rosy Apple Aphid. Rosy apple aphid (*Dysaphis plantaginea*) is potentially the most damaging aphid species affecting apples.

Seasonal Development. Rosy apple aphid overwinters as shiny, black oval eggs on the bark of twigs and spurs of apple trees. Nymphs hatch in spring at bud swell and feed on expanding buds, moving to leaves of developing fruit clusters before becoming reproductive adults. These founding females are called *stem mothers* and give birth to live nymphs without mating. They colonize new growth inside the curled leaves. Nymphs vary in color from dark green to purple and often have a dust-like, gray wax covering the body. They have very long cornicles.

By late June or July the aphids develop wings and migrate to plantain where they spend the summer. In the fall they migrate back to the apples, where they mate and lay eggs on fruiting spurs and shoots.

Symptoms. Rosy apple aphids form colonies on leaves of fruiting spurs and shoots where their feeding causes the leaves to curl (see color plate 3.8). Fruit on heavily infested spurs become bumpy, distorted, and stunted. The damage results from a toxin in the saliva injected by the aphid while feeding. Damaged shoots may be permanently stunted, which is particularly detrimental in young, developing orchards.

Monitoring and Control. Collect 100 fruit spurs from different parts of trees throughout the orchard and examine them for rosy apple aphid eggs. If eggs are found, plan on applying a dormant or delayed dormant spray, as described below.

The preferred control for rosy apple aphid is the application of a delayed dormant oil spray (1 to 8 percent) applied within 2 weeks of green tip. The application of a dormant oil spray (8 percent) in January will also help to control overwintering eggs and may be worthwhile if limited orchard access during the delayed dormant period is expected due to rain.

Naturally occurring generalist predators (lady beetle adults and larvae, syrphid fly larvae, lacewing larvae) and some parasitoids can be effective in controlling rosy apple aphid. However, populations of predators may not reach effective levels in spring until after significant aphid damage has occurred. Augmentative releases of predators have not proven to be effective. They may disperse rapidly from the release orchard, their development to the predatory stage after release may be limited by climatic factors (lacewings), they may not establish well in California orchards (*Aphidoletes aphidimyza*), or they may not be available from insectaries (syrphid flies). Control by parasitoids is generally low and may not occur until later in the season.

It is difficult to control rosy apple aphid during the growing season because the colonies are protected inside the curled leaves. However, a supplemental spring treatment of organically acceptable spray materials may be warranted if aphid pressure is high. Examine leaves and clusters in 20 trees per block beginning at first petal fall. If leaf curling and aphids are found and predation or parasitism is not evident, additional in-season sprays may be needed. No exact thresholds have been established. If predators or parasitoids are feeding on aphid colonies, it may be worthwhile to wait several days to see if they are keeping the aphid populations below damaging levels before sprays are applied.

Summer oil (2 percent) has proven to be effective in reducing shoot damage when applied at the first sign of symptoms (usually around petal fall) and reapplied two to three times at 10-day intervals as long as active infestations are found. The addition of Neemix (0.5 gal/acre [4.7 L/ha]) to the summer oil improves the control. To be effective, the oil must be applied under high pressure to ensure small particle size and good coverage. Note that these sprays can be damaging to some beneficial insects, so they should only be used if the beneficials are not evident or not keeping the aphids in check. Other organic materials, such as insec-

ticidal soap, pyrethrum, and neem (without the summer oil) have not been effective in controlling rosy apple aphid.

An in-season aphid control program may be difficult to coordinate with an apple scab control program in areas that typically experience prolonged spring rains. Lime sulfur is often added to the delayed dormant oil spray at green tip to control scab. However, after green tip, oil and sulfur or lime sulfur should not be applied within 3 weeks of each other. This requires the organic grower to anticipate which problem may cause the most damage and often to treat for that problem at the expense of the other.

Fixed copper sprays for apple scab control do not interact in the same way as sulfur products and oils to cause burning. Thus, oil and fixed copper sprays may be another option for coordinated apple scab and aphid control. However, copper may cause fruit russeting if applied after bloom.

Any shoot damage should be pruned out during the growing season after aphids are gone to encourage the growth of replacement wood. This is particularly important in young, developing orchards.

Ants protect aphids from predators and move aphid colonies throughout the orchard, increasing damage and prolonging the infestation. Organic growers may want to control ants with a sticky substance, such as Tanglefoot, applied to tree trunks, or with approved baits (such as boric acid) during the growing season (to prevent damage the following spring) or early in the season before aphid populations are apparent.

Woolly Apple Aphid. Woolly apple aphid (*Eriosoma lanigerum*) infests roots, trunk, limbs, shoots, and, occasionally fruit. The reddish to purple bodies of these mostly bark-feeding aphids are completely covered with white, wool-like waxy material. This aphid is most often a problem in coastal counties but is found in all California apple-growing districts.

Seasonal Development. This aphid is found in colonies on the aerial portions of the tree and on roots in winter. Large numbers of nymphs are produced by both aerial and root colonies beginning in early summer and continuing into fall. Then the nymphs migrate up or down the trunks of infested trees during summer and fall. The root habitat and migration make their control difficult.

Symptoms. Woolly apple aphids inhabiting the above-ground portions of the tree colonize old pruning wounds and scars at the base of buds. The main injury to young trees is stunting caused by formation of root galls, which also may be present on mature trees. Once established, however, the tree is less affected. Large aerial galls are often present on mature trees, Winter Banana being among the most susceptible varieties. When populations are extremely large, honeydew and sooty mold develop. Woolly apple aphids may also enter the calyx end of fruits, especially the Yellow Newtown variety, and cause contamination by insect parts in processed apple products. The Malling, or "M" series of rootstocks with numbers over 100 are resistant to this pest.

Root colonies cause the greatest damage because galling renders the root nonfunctional, retarding tree growth. Rootstocks are affected differently, depending on genetics and environment. Roots of trees growing in heavy clay soils are usually more extensively infested than those growing in sandy soils.

Control. A parasitic wasp (*Aphelinus mali*) attacks and can completely control the aerial colonies. Parasitized aphids are black and may have an exit hole from which a parasite emerged. Brown and green lacewings, lady beetles, and syrphid fly larvae regulate woolly apple aphid populations. Predators can destroy entire colonies, and outbreaks have been blamed on pesticide applications that disrupted this biological control.

Delayed dormant oil sprays may provide moderate control of aerial forms. Where woolly apple aphid is a serious problem use resistant rootstocks of the Malling-Merton series (MM111 and MM106).

Green Apple Aphid. Green apple aphid (*Aphis pomi*) infests succulent terminal growth, and in heavy infestations it is also found on fruit.

Seasonal Development. Overwintering eggs are found on twigs of the previous season's growth and on fruit spurs. The eggs are identical in appearance to rosy apple aphid eggs: shiny, black, and oval. They hatch just before bloom as the first leaves are unfolding. Stem mothers produce live young without mating. Newly hatched apple aphids are dark green, and mature aphids on apple foliage in spring and summer are bright yellow-green. Winged adults that can spread infestations to other trees have a black head and thorax and a yellow-green abdomen with darker green lateral spots. In late fall, small, dusky, yellow wingless males and normal-sized, yellow-brown wingless females develop. Females lay tiny, oval overwintering eggs. This aphid remains on apples throughout the growing season with no alternate hosts; they can have ten or more generations a year. Populations tend to decline when temperatures exceed 95°F (35°C).

Symptoms. High populations of green apple aphids on young trees may seriously retard normal growth and result in irregular shoot growth. On bearing trees, heavy infestations of aphids may cover the fruit and foliage with honeydew on which a sooty black fungus develops. The black sticky coating hinders normal leaf function and can lower the grade of fruit.

Control. A delayed dormant oil spray to control overwintering eggs is the most effective treatment when predators are absent or ineffective. Management of nitrogen fertility and irrigation to reduce shoot growth helps to slow aphid population growth rates. Additional control is not required unless trees are severely infested (more than 60 percent of shoots affected). When population levels are this high, they may be organically controlled with insecticidal soap, summer oil, or Neemix sprays.

Mites

Seasonal Development. European red mite (*Panonychus ulmi*) can produce numerous generations from the late pink bud stage through September. Overwintering eggs are tiny, red, somewhat flattened globes, with a spine projecting from the top. They may be present in large numbers on small branches and in cracks on fruit spurs. Newly hatched mites are bright red, and older stages are usually dark red with whitish spots at the base of the spines on the back. This mite prefers to feed on the upper side of the leaf.

The two-spotted mite (*Tetranychus urticae*) lives on alternate hosts in spring; then populations increase in early summer when they infest apple trees. These mites are first noticed on the lower sides of leaves at the center of the tree, having moved up the trunk from surrounding vegetation. They eventually spread to the entire tree. Warm weather favors their development. Adult female two-spotted mites are larger and more elongated than European red mites and are green to yellow. Feeding mites have a dark spot on either side of the body that may enlarge to cover most of the body. The tiny, spherical, colorless to light straw-colored eggs are distributed over the infested area. Overwintering females are orange and do not have spots; they develop in fall and seek hibernation quarters. Two-spotted mites spin a characteristic webbing over leaves and twigs when populations are high.

Other mites such as McDaniel (*T. mcdanieli*) and Pacific (*T. pacificus*) can also attack apple trees.

Symptoms and Damage. Mites of the above species remove the cell contents from leaves, gradually giving the leaf a finely mottled or stippled appearance. Heavy infestation results in severe bronzing of foliage and premature defoliation. Fruits on heavily infested trees fail to size and color properly, and fruit production for the following year may also be lowered. Such varieties as Red Delicious, Golden Delicious, Rome Beauty, and Jonathan are very susceptible to mite injury, while Gravenstein and Yellow Newtown show less evidence of leaf damage from moderate populations.

Control. Dormant and delayed dormant sprays (see aphid controls, above) are common preventive control measures in organically managed orchards. Mites are rarely an economic problem in well-managed organic apple orchards as long as dormant sprays are used consistently and trees are kept well watered to avoid moisture stress. Mite natural enemies, mostly predators such as the western predatory mite, green lacewings, ladybird beetles, and minuter pirate bugs, are not disturbed under normal organic management. Additional preventive measures include reducing dust by limiting traffic in the orchard and watering roads.

Leafrollers

Leafrollers, also known as skinworms and tortricids, are caterpillars belonging to the family Tortricidae. There are five species of concern to apple growers in California: obliquebanded leafroller (*Choristoneura rosaceana*), apple pandemis (*Pandemis pyrusana*), orange tortrix (*Argyrotaenia citrana*), fruittree leafroller (*Archips argyrospila*), and omnivorous leafroller (*Platynota stultana*). The obliquebanded and fruittree leafrollers are present in all apple districts in California, although obliquebanded leafroller is primarily an inland and Sierra Foothills pest. Omnivorous leafroller is primarily a problem in the interior valley and foothills and is not present in the coastal areas. Orange tortrix is primarily a pest in coastal areas (Watsonville, Sonoma) although it is occasionally found in the interior valley. Apple pandemis is only found in coastal areas, primarily the Central Coast.

Symptoms and Damage. Leafroller larvae and damage are quite characteristic. Early in the year, during the pink stage just before bloom, obliquebanded leafroller, apple pandemis, and fruittree leafroller larvae begin feeding on leaves and buds. Shallow pitting may result and may heal over into a small, scaly scar. As they grow, the larvae web or roll leaves to form a protected site and then feed on the leaf or skin of the developing fruit. Leaves may show small square or rectangular light brown areas called *window panes* left by the feeding on the underside of the leaf. The caterpillar is quite active and will wiggle backwards when disturbed and drop from a slender silk thread.

Later damage by all species of leafrollers (except the fruittree leafroller) is characterized by tunneling, pitting, or gouging of the skin (hence the name skinworms). Near harvest, they can also cause small pinhole damage that looks much like a codling moth sting. These holes usually occur where two fruit come in contact or a leaf lays on the fruit. Unlike codling moth, however, leafrollers do not bore into the center of the fruit. Fruittree leafroller has only one generation per year and only damages fruit during spring. As moths, these insects do not feed on leaves or fruit. Table 3.6 presents common field characteristics and damage periods by leafrollers of concern to apple growers.

Monitoring Larvae. The most reliable method of monitoring for damage levels of leafrollers is to look

Table 3.6. Some common field characteristics of leafrollers found in apples.

Common name (location in state)	Larval identification	Crop hosts	Time of damage
Apple pandemis (coastal)	green larvae, pale or gold head	apples, caneberries	bloom, early to midsummer
Obliquebanded leafroller (coastal, interior)	green larvae, dark black or brown head	apples, pears, apricots, pistachios, California buckeye	bloom, June–July, and late at harvest
Orange tortrix (mostly coastal)	yellow-green larvae, gold head	apples, pears, stone fruits, grapes, berries, weeds	June–July, September–October
Fruittree leafroller (coastal, interior)	green larvae, black head	apples, pears, most stone fruits and nuts, *Ribes* spp., California buckeye, some ornamental trees, citrus	bloom
Omnivorous leafroller (interior)	yellow-green larvae with elliptical tubercles on dorsum, dark brown head capsule (early instars); light brown head capsule (late instars)	apples, pears, stone fruits, caneberries, grapes, citrus, alfalfa	June–harvest

for larvae. At bloom, walk through the orchard and randomly pick one flower cluster off each of 100 trees for every 10 to 20 acres (4 to 8 ha). If leaves are already coming out, alternate between flower clusters and leaf clusters, as the larvae quickly move to young leaves. A damaged cluster typically has several ragged buds stuck together. The presence of webbing and small black fecal pellets in the cluster or several leaves stuck or webbed together at the end of a new shoot may indicate leafroller feeding.

During summer, one or more checks for leafroller larvae may be advisable, especially if the orchard has a history of leafroller problems. Larvae can be monitored by walking through the orchard and visually checking trees for leaves that are webbed together and have the telltale windowpane damage (webbed leaves can also be indicative of spiders and earwigs). Pay special attention to short-stemmed varieties that grow in tight clusters, such as Yellow Newtowns and Gravensteins, and to poorly thinned fruit where a great number of fruit are touching.

Monitoring Adults. Monitoring adult moths helps track leafroller development, but this is only possible if the species has distinct, separate generations. Orange tortrix and omnivorous leafroller have several overlapping generations, and fruittree leafroller is only harmful as larvae at bloom, so monitoring adults of these species is not very effective. The two species worth monitoring with pheromone traps are apple pandemis (coastal areas) and obliquebanded leafroller.

In spring, set out cardboard sticky traps (similar to those used for codling moth) with commercial pheromone baits to attract apple pandemis or obliquebanded leafroller. Check the traps once a week, removing any moths and recording the number found. About two weeks to one month after peak moth flight is the time to look for larvae. Pheromone traps are NOT good predictors of larval density or fruit damage because moths from outside the orchard are attracted to the traps.

Cultural Controls. Leafrollers tend to cause more damage to short-stemmed apples and fruit in tight clusters. Hand thinning the fruit to reduce the number of apples per cluster can help control leafrollers by removing their preferred habitat. Early harvest can help avoid buildup of orange tortrix during September and October.

Microbial Controls. If you find leafroller larvae during spring, consider applying a *Bacillus thuringiensis* (Bt) product to control the pests, particularly if the fruit is intended for the fresh market. In spring, a fruit or leaf infestation of 1 percent for obliquebanded leafroller and 2 percent for fruittree leafroller generally warrants spring treatment. A minimum of 100 clusters should be examined per 20-acre (8-ha) block. It may

not be cost-effective to apply Bt early in the season on apples intended for processing.

Natural enemies and other factors often keep leafroller populations low in organic orchards, so Bt applications are cost effective and only advisable if the number of leafroller larvae is high. There are several Bt products available that are compatible with organic production methods. The threshold for treatment depends on the particular production requirements of the grower. Omnivorous leafroller is not a severe pest of apples, and control is seldom needed.

Because of the leaf rolling habit of this group of moths, timing the insecticide applications is extremely important. Bt is organically acceptable, but once the worms roll the leaf, this treatment will not provide control. Control is best when Bt is applied in spring as leaves are just expanding, which ensures the worm will feed on microbial control material.

When using Bt products, remember that they break down within about 3 days in the orchard (even sooner with rain). Therefore, only apply the product if larvae are present. Bt sprays have no effect on adult moths. Apply Bt two or three times at 1-week intervals, and try to time your applications to coincide with warm, sunny weather. Apply Bt at label rates using a conventional volume spray. Do not mix Bt products with alkaline materials such as lime sulfur because alkaline materials cause Bt to break down. Also, Bt must be eaten by the larvae to kill them, so any additives that might discourage feeding will reduce the product's effectiveness.

Dormant Oils. A dormant oil application, which should always be applied for San Jose scale, various apple aphids, and European red mite, provides the best control of fruittree leafroller. If applied correctly, a minimum of 6 gallons per acre (56 L/ha) of a dormant oil minimizes damage from this pest.

Biological Controls. There are a number of parasitoids that attack leafrollers, including several species of parasitic wasps and a tachinid fly. As with parasitoids of the other species, biological control is variable from year to year and may not provide adequate population reduction. There are no recorded parasitoids of fruittree leafroller, although natural control is provided to some extent by generalist predators.

Tentiform Leafminer

Description and Symptoms. The leafminer (*Phyllonorycter mespilella*) is found throughout the Pacific Northwest. The larvae have two different forms: sap feeders and tissue feeders. In the earlier sap-feeding stage, the larvae separate the outer layer of the leaf undersurface from the tissue above by creating a snakelike mine that enlarges to a blotch. The mines left by a leafminer in sap-feeding stage are always flat and visible only on the lower surface of leaves. Later, in the tissue-feeding stage, larvae feed on the upper part of the leaf tissue. As a result, chewing holes can be seen on the upper leaf surface. The tissue-feeding larvae also tie the sides of the mine together with silk, arching the mine and giving it its characteristic tentiform appearance.

Pupation takes place within a silk cocoon inside the mine. The pupa is cylindrical, tapering toward the rear, and darkens from light tan to dark brown as it develops. The adult is small (about ¼ inch [6.5 mm] long) with gold-bronze wings marked by a white streak edged with black. At rest, wings are held roof-like over the body.

Seasonal Development. Adult leafminer moths emerge in late February, or later in foothill districts. Female moths mate and begin laying eggs when the first leaves are unfolding. The first generation develops in the fruiting spur leaves and completes its development from late April to early May. In subsequent generations, females lay eggs in the younger, fully expanded leaves of the shoot. The second generation completes its development between June and July, and later generations overlap. After leaf fall, tentiform leafminers overwinter as pupae within the tissue of the fallen leaves.

Damage. Infestations greater than 5 to 10 mines per leaf may lead to premature defoliation, causing sunburning of the fruit. Even if defoliation does not occur, high populations in late summer can damage enough leaf tissue to reduce fruit size, sugars, and color.

Biological Control. Populations of leafminers are usually kept at low levels in organic orchards by several naturally occurring parasitic wasps, particularly *Pnigalio flavipes* and *Sympiesis marylandensis*. These parasites are easily disrupted by broad-spectrum insecticide sprays, and leafminers often become problematic in orchards where these materials are used.

Female parasites lay their eggs inside the leaf mine. After hatching, the parasitic larvae attach to the leafminer larvae, feeding on them until the leafminer is consumed. The parasite pupates inside the mine. Adult parasites emerge from the mine by cutting a round hole in the leaf tissue. Parasitism at levels above 30 percent during the first and second generations will keep leafminer densities at low levels.

VERTEBRATE PEST MANAGEMENT

Pocket gophers and meadow mice are the most common vertebrate pests in apple orchards. Other species that may cause problems include ground squirrels, deer, rabbits, and birds. In addition to damaging fruit, mammals can cause long-term damage by killing or seriously stunting trees. The burrowing activity of pocket gophers and ground squirrels can also interfere with management activities such as mowing and irrigation. Coyotes may be of concern in some areas due to their habit of chewing on drip irrigation lines. In some orchards, birds may be the most serious problem as several species can reduce fruit yield by feeding on flower buds and ripening fruit.

The vertebrate pest problems in a given orchard are determined in large part by the orchard's location. Problems are often worse in orchards that are adjacent to rangeland or unmanaged areas where pest populations are not controlled. Orchard management activities also have some effect on vertebrate pest problems; for example, flood irrigation and orchard floor cultivation may discourage meadow mouse populations.

Management Guidelines

The most successful approach to managing vertebrate pests is to maintain pest populations at levels where significant damage does not occur. This preventive approach is of particular importance in organic orchards where the options for reducing damaging populations are limited to labor intensive techniques such as shooting or trapping. Regular monitoring of vertebrate pests in and around apple orchards should form the basis of a management program. Historical records of pest population levels, control methods implemented, and their effects can be used to help determine the best management approach.

Correct identification of the species causing damage is critical for choosing appropriate control actions. Signs such as tracks, feces, and burrows may be used to identify different species. Where birds are a problem, direct observation is needed to distinguish between harmless species that frequent orchards and those species that actually cause damage.

For most vertebrate pests, more than one control method is usually available to manage damaging populations, although their relative effectiveness may vary. For some of the most serious pests such as gophers and ground squirrels, all efforts should be made to bring their populations under control prior to organic certification. Table 3.7 lists control options that may be used for important vertebrate pests. Each of these options is discussed in more detail below.

Biological Control

Vertebrate populations are affected most by availability of food and cover, while diseases and predators play a relatively minor role. A number of predators such as hawks, owls, foxes, coyotes, and snakes feed on some of the vertebrate pest species. However, natural enemies seldom keep vertebrate pests from reaching damaging levels so they should not be relied on to prevent vertebrates from causing economic damage to crops. Factors that limit the role of predators in rodent control include

- the tendency of predators to modify their diets according to the relative abundance of prey species

- the high reproductive rate of small rodents that allows their populations to compensate for loss to predation

- predator avoidance strategies developed by prey species

In some instances, predators may actually be detrimental to production. For example, coyotes frequently chew on and damage drip lines. If their presence poses no hazard, however, predators may be considered a small component of an integrated management program. Growers in favorable settings can enhance the orchard habitat (through installation of nest boxes, raptor perches, and so on) to increase the probability that these predators will use the rodent prey base in the orchard. However, growers should be aware that there is little or no data to suggest that the installation of nest boxes or raptor perches has any measurable effect on pest rodent populations. One study showed that despite quick acceptance of perches and an increase in raptors in the areas studied, rodent numbers did not change.

Principal Vertebrate Pests

***Pocket Gophers* (Thomomys bottae).** Pocket gophers can be serious pests, especially in young orchards. Pocket gophers feed on the bark of tree crowns and roots, girdling and killing young trees and reducing the vigor of older trees. Damage is usually below ground and often is not evident until trees show signs of stress. Damage to drip lines and diversion of water through burrow systems may also be problems.

Food quantity and quality are major factors influencing the distribution and abundance of pocket gophers throughout their range. As breeding is regulated by the availability of green forage, high density populations may be associated with the presence of cover crops such as perennial clovers. Consequently, tree damage under these situations may be quite severe.

Management Guidelines. Fan-shaped mounds are the most obvious sign of the presence of gophers. Gopher activity should be monitored monthly in late fall, winter, and spring, with close attention given to orchard perimeters where gophers may move in from adjacent infested areas. Monitoring is especially important in orchards with ground covers because they are more likely to support gophers, and the presence of vegetation may make burrowing activity harder to detect.

Controls should be implemented as soon as gopher activity is detected and while the population is at a manageable level. Gophers also should be controlled on orchard perimeters and in adjacent areas to reduce

Table 3.7. Control options for important vertebrate pests in organic apple orchards.

Pest	Habitat modification	Trapping	Fencing	Tree protectors	Frightening	Shooting
Pocket gophers	x	x				
Meadow mice	x			x		
Ground squirrels	x	x				x
Rabbits	x		x	x		x
Deer	x		x	x	x	x
Birds	x	x			x	x

Note: The certification agency California Certified Organic Farmers (CCOF) no longer allows use of strychnine to control pocket gophers.

the potential for invasion. Techniques include site preparation to reduce the initial population of gophers, consideration of cultural practices including the type and blend of cover crop planted, and increased attention given to monitoring and control efforts. In adjacent, uncertified areas, growers should consider using pesticides to reduce the number of gophers that may potentially invade the orchard.

Habitat modification. Gophers should be controlled by deep plowing and trapping prior to planting an orchard. As most of a pocket gopher's burrow system is from 8 to 12 inches (21 to 31 cm) below the ground, deep plowing and disking can destroy much of the burrow system, as well as kill some of the pocket gophers.

Clean cultivation of the orchard floor reduces the food supply and destroys burrows, making the orchard less habitable for gophers. Clean cultivation also makes it easier to monitor gopher activity. Where cover cropping is practiced and gophers are more likely to be a problem, care should be taken to choose a cover crop blend not favored by gophers. Pocket gophers prefer fleshy and succulent roots and stems of herbaceous annual and perennial plants (alfalfa, clovers) over grasses having fibrous root systems. Cover crops that consist of grasses or cereals with fibrous root systems (barley, rye, annual ryegrass, foxtail fescue) rather than taprooted legumes (clovers, bell beans) may limit the amount of forage available to pocket gophers and thereby reduce the potential for large populations to develop. It is important to note that some grasses high in moisture content (such as California brome) are favored by pocket gophers and also should be avoided.

Trapping. Although labor intensive and therefore relatively expensive, trapping is the only effective management technique available to organic growers. Trapping is most effective if undertaken systematically and when the population is relatively low. Having sufficient trappers and traps to conduct an intensive trapping program in a few months is critical to the success of this method. Trapping is most effective if undertaken in the fall when mound building activity peaks. Either pincer or box traps can be used. They are placed in the main tunnel of a pocket gopher burrow, which is usually 8 to 12 inches (21 to 31 cm) deep and located by probing near a fresh mound. Traps should be placed in pairs, one facing each direction, and anchored with wire to a stake. Traps should be checked daily. If a trap is not visited within 48 hours by a gopher, it should be moved to a new location.

Meadow Mice (Microtus spp.). Meadow mice, also called voles or meadow voles, forage almost exclusively aboveground on fresh leaves and stems of a wide variety of grasses and broadleaf plants. Seeds, woody materials, and bark also are taken. Small trees are usually the most susceptible to being completely girdled at the base and killed by mice, but even mature trees can be damaged severely or killed. Populations and damage are usually highest in orchards where dense vegetation is allowed to build up around tree bases. Maintaining vegetation-free areas around the base of trees is the key control method for meadow mice and usually keeps damage to a minimum.

Management Guidelines. Meadow mouse populations are cyclical and may change from very low, almost undetectable populations to high numbers in just a few months. This often catches the grower unaware. Monitoring should be undertaken monthly during winter and spring when populations are most likely to be increasing. Fresh mouse droppings and short pieces of clipped vegetation, especially grass stems, in runways are indicators of the presence of meadow mice. If these signs are found, trees should be checked for bark damage. Meadow mice usually start chewing on the bark about 2 inches (5 cm) below the soil line, then move upward. Ditchbanks, fencerows, and other areas near the orchard where permanent vegetation is favorable for the buildup of mouse populations should also be monitored.

Habitat modification. Ground vegetation provides food, concealment from predators, and protection from unfavorable weather. It is the most important factor affecting meadow mouse abundance. An area of about 3 feet (1 m) out from the tree trunk should be kept free of vegetation to discourage meadow mice from living at the base of the trees. If ground cover is maintained in the row middles, frequent close mowing will remove protective cover. Mowing may also have a short-term effect by disturbing populations and causing individual mice to disperse. However, it is important to note that clippings left as a dense thatch layer on the ground are likely to improve the habitat for mice by affording them more protection. Similarly, mulches may be used as cover by meadow mice, resulting in tree damage just below the mulch layer. If meadow mice become a problem, mulches should be avoided. If their numbers increase substantially, clean cultivation by disking and maintaining vegetation-free tree rows are critical.

Where meadow mice are likely to be a problem, careful consideration should be given to the type of cover crop planted. Dense covers that form a continuous canopy support high populations. By contrast, plants with erect, bunch-type growth or covers that reach a short mature height with reduced mowing requirements and increased light penetration at ground level provide mice with little protective cover.

Practices that reduce cover in surrounding areas also can play a role in preventing serious meadow mouse problems. These practices include controlling weeds; cultivating fence rows, roadsides, and ditch-banks; and reducing ground cover in adjacent orchards. Such areas often provide a habitat from which meadow mice invade an orchard.

Tree protectors. Wire trunk guards can be used to protect young trees from mice. However, if not used correctly the protectors may give a false sense of protection. They should only be used where vegetation is controlled at the base of the tree. The most effective guards are cylinders made from ¼-inch (6.5-mm) or ½-inch (12.5-mm) hardware cloth that is 24 inches (61 cm) wide and of sufficient diameter to allow several years of growth without crowding the tree. Guards should be buried at least 6 inches (15 cm) below the soil surface to discourage mice from burrowing under them. Plastic, cardboard, or other fibrous materials are less expensive but do not provide the same degree of protection. If these materials are used, they should be checked periodically because mice may burrow underneath them to gnaw on the tree trunk.

Ground Squirrels (Spermophilus beecheyi).

Ground squirrels feed on ripening fruit and damage trees by chewing bark off limbs and tree trunks. Burrow systems in the orchard may interfere with orchard management activities and divert irrigation water. Problems also result when ground squirrels chew on and damage drip lines. California ground squirrels tend to disappear from land that is under complete and frequent cultivation. However, they maintain burrow systems along berms, fence lines, road rights-of-way, and in other suitable uncultivated areas. They travel 100 yards (91 m) or more to feed in adjacent crops. Following their spring emergence from hibernation, ground squirrels feed almost exclusively on green vegetation. When annual grasses and forbes start to produce seeds and dry up, squirrels begin eating seeds, fruits, and bark from vines and trees.

Management Guidelines. Squirrel activity should be monitored periodically both inside and on the perimeter of the orchard in spring, summer, and fall when squirrels are active. Midmorning is usually the best time of day to observe squirrel activity. Controls should be implemented as soon as burrowing activity is first observed in order to keep numbers from increasing. Where large numbers of squirrels are moving into the orchard to feed, trapping along the perimeter offers the most effective control. Provided regulations pertaining to buffer strips are followed, toxic baits should be used in the summer to control squirrels on uncertified land and prevent squirrels from moving into orchards. Fumigants may also be applied to burrows in late winter or early spring in these areas. Fumigants are especially useful because they reduce the breeding population.

Habitat modification. Removing brush piles, stumps, and debris in and around the orchard may help limit buildup of squirrel populations to some extent and make it easier to monitor squirrel activity. Squirrels may quickly reinvade abandoned burrow systems. On orchard perimeters, deep plowing, where practical, to destroy burrow entrances will help slow down the rate of invasion.

Trapping. Trapping is a highly effective control method. It is far less labor intensive than trapping for gophers and can easily be undertaken by one individual. With ample traps and a concentrated effort, even a moderate population of squirrels over a large area can be brought under control. Trapping can be undertaken at any time of year when squirrels are active but is most effective in spring before reproduction increases the population. The most commonly used traps are kill traps such as the Conibear trap or box traps.

Conibear traps are placed unbaited over the burrow entrance and trap squirrels as they exit. Within the range of the San Joaquin kit fox, the trap must be placed in a covered box with an entrance no larger than 3 inches (7.5 cm) wide to exclude the fox. Box traps are also effective for ground squirrels and are baited with walnuts, almonds, oats, barley, or melon rinds. The bait is placed inside the trap, either behind the trigger or tied to it.

Black-Tailed Jackrabbits/Cottontail and Brush Rabbits.

Rabbits may cause severe damage to young trees by chewing the bark off the trunk and clipping off branches within their reach to eat buds and young foliage. They also may gnaw on drip irrigation lines. While black-tailed jackrabbits (*Lepus californicus*) are the most common problem, cottontail and brush rabbits (*Sylvilagus* spp.) may damage trees in orchards near the more wooded or brushy habitats favored by these species.

Rabbits are active all year in fruit-growing areas. They often live outside of orchards, moving in to feed from early evening to early morning. Damage to trees occurs primarily in winter and early spring when other sources of food are limited. Once the orchard is 4 or 5 years old, rabbits usually are not a serious problem. Damage can be prevented with proper use of fencing or tree guards. Trapping and shooting may also be used.

Management Guidelines. New plantings should be examined periodically for damage by rabbits. Bark damage usually extends higher on the tree than that caused by meadow mice, and tooth marks are distinctly larger. Droppings and tracks can also be used to determine if rabbits are the cause of damage. Where damage occurs, orchard perimeters should be monitored in early morning or late evening to see where rabbits are entering and to obtain an estimate of the number of rabbits involved.

Fencing. Rabbit-proof fencing around the entire orchard is the most effective way to prevent damage to young trees in locations where rabbits are a major concern. The fence should be made of woven wire or poultry netting at least 3 feet (90 cm) wide with a mesh diameter of 1 inch (2.5 cm) or less. Bend the bottom 6 inches (15 cm) of mesh outwards at a 90-degree angle and bury it 6 inches deep facing away from the orchard to prevent rabbits from digging under the fence. The cost of a rabbit fence that may only be needed for a few years may be prohibitive for large orchards. Tree protectors are an alternative.

Tree protectors. Tree protectors are a practical way to prevent damage when a few trees are being replanted in an established orchard. They can be made from wire mesh, hardware cloth, plastic, paper, or cardboard. Cylinders made from poultry netting or hardware cloth and secured with stakes or wooden spreaders offer the best protection against rabbits. The cylinder should be at least 2.5 feet (0.76 m) high so that jackrabbits cannot reach foliage and limbs by standing on their back legs.

Other methods. Shooting is a highly effective method for controlling rabbits and should be undertaken in the early morning and during the evening when they are most active. If small numbers of rabbits are involved, shooting may be all that is necessary to prevent significant damage when trees are young. Trapping may provide effective control for small populations of rabbits or may be used to reduce damage temporarily until other measures such as fencing or tree guards can be put in place. Box-type or similar traps can be an effective way to control small populations of cottontail or brush rabbits. Trapping is not effective for jackrabbits because they do not enter traps readily. Removing brush piles from perimeters of orchards may reduce rabbit populations by removing shelter.

Mule Deer (Odocoileus hemionus). Deer can be a serious pest of newly planted trees in some foothill and coastal orchards and in the Central Valley near riparian habitat. Young trees can be severely stunted, deformed, and killed by deer browsing on new shoots. Deer also feed on the new growth of older trees, but this seldom causes significant damage. Bucks occasionally break limbs or injure bark when they use trees to rub the velvet off their antlers.

Management Guidelines. If deer are causing significant damage, deer-proof fencing provides the most effective and lasting control. Fencing is most effective at excluding deer when it is put in place before planting the orchard. Fencing must be at least 7 feet (2.1 m) high to exclude deer. On sloping terrain, an 8-foot (2.4-m) high or taller fence may be necessary. Woven wire fences or high tensile electric fences are commonly used.

Wire mesh cylinders around individual trees may be an effective option where a few new trees are being planted in a location subject to deer damage. The cylinders should be at least 4 feet (1.2 m) tall, of sufficient diameter that deer cannot reach over them to the foliage, and secured with wooden stakes so they cannot be tipped over.

Other controls. Habitat management is usually not an option for controlling deer because they travel long distances to reach food sources. Noise-making devices may be effective for a few days, but deer become accustomed to them quickly. Depredation permits sometimes will be issued by the California Department of Fish and Game to shoot animals that are causing damage. This may be necessary if a deer gets inside a fenced orchard and is not able to escape. Shooting will not solve a serious deer problem, but it may prevent damage long enough to allow construction of a fence.

Birds. Birds can cause substantial damage by feeding on ripening fruit. This is usually most severe in orchards adjacent to wild or brushy areas where birds find refuge, breeding sites, and other food sources. Orchards surrounded by other orchards tend to have fewer problems with birds.

Management Guidelines. Regular monitoring is important to help determine when damage actually starts so that control actions can be initiated early. Birds are much more difficult to control once they have become used to feeding in a particular orchard. To monitor the occurrence of bird damage, it is easier to watch for the movement of birds into or within the orchard than to detect the damage itself. This is particularly true of bud damage in winter, which is difficult to see and may go undetected until bloom. Bud damage usually occurs in the upper parts of trees on the margins of an orchard, next to brushy or wooded habitat from which flocks of house finches or crowned sparrows move into the orchard. Bird activity should be monitored on a weekly basis where damage is suspected.

Frightening devices (noisemakers and visual repellents) are the primary means of controlling bird damage in apple orchards, but unfortunately they produce limited results. Trapping can be effective for house finches and starlings. Removal of brush piles that offer refuge and resting sites for birds in or near orchards may reduce problems.

Frightening. The most effective way to frighten birds from the orchard is to use a combination of noisemakers and visual repellents. Rotating between types and combinations of frightening devices so that birds do not habituate as rapidly to the sound or visual repellent is most effective.

Roving patrols that fire shell crackers, bird bombs, or whistler bombs are one of the most effective ways to frighten birds from orchards. Stationary noisemakers such as gas cannons (propane exploders) and electronic noisemakers are most effective with at least one device for every 5 acres (2 ha) and when they are elevated above the level of the tree canopy. The devices should be moved to new locations every 3 to 5 days so the birds take longer to get used to them. The most commonly used visual repellents are large "scare-eye" balloons and Mylar streamers.

Shooting. Birds that usually invade orchards in small numbers, such as scrub jays and magpies, often can be controlled by shooting. Permits are not presently required to shoot crows, magpies, or starlings that are causing damage, but local authorities should be consulted prior to any bird shooting because regulations may change. A depredation permit is required to shoot scrub jays. Where permissible, occasionally shooting at a few birds will increase the effectiveness of other noise-making techniques, because the birds will begin associating loud noises with the real hazards of being shot at.

Trapping. Trapping can be an effective way to control house finches and starlings, especially if it is conducted over a relatively large area, for example, if several adjacent growers conduct a trapping program. The most effective trap for these species is the modified Australian crow trap. Successful trapping must take into account the behavior patterns of the birds being controlled. For example, both nest-box and decoy traps may be used for trapping starlings. However, nest-box traps are successful only during the nesting season, whereas decoy traps are effective during other times when starlings are flocking. For house finches and crowned sparrows, trapping must be done under the supervision of the County Agricultural Commissioner.

4

Harvest and Postharvest Operations

The entire harvest and postharvest handling system must be carefully managed to optimize the quality and storage life of organic apples. Many cultural practices are important factors:

- tree training, irrigation, and nutrition

- harvesting at optimum maturity

- sanitation in the orchard and packinghouse

- careful handling to prevent fruit injury

- rapid cooling after harvest and storage at the lowest safe temperature

- controlled atmosphere storage

No one single factor can provide assurance of postharvest quality, but many factors must be considered as part of the entire harvest-postharvest system. *Commercial Apple Growing in California* (ANR Publication 2456, 1992) provides an excellent overview of physiology and pathology of apples during and after harvest, as well as maturity standards, harvesting operations, cooling, storage, and packing house operations. Included below are those additional considerations important to organic production.

PREHARVEST FACTORS

Cultivars differ considerably in their susceptibility to various postharvest disorders. For example, Granny Smith and Red Delicious are very susceptible to storage scald, and Granny Smith, Red Delicious, and Golden Delicious are very susceptible to bitter pit.

Cultural practices within an established orchard are important determinants of postharvest quality. Nutritional factors affect fruit firmness, storage life, and susceptibility to decay and physiological disorders. In general, high fruit nitrogen or low fruit calcium leads to poor quality fruit. Fertilization practices should be designed to prevent excessive fruit nitrogen and to enhance fruit calcium content as much as possible. Fruit that is too large can have decreased calcium levels. Cultural practices that avoid light crop loads and large fruit will improve fruit calcium status and reduce susceptibility to physiological disorders and decay (see discussion of bitter pit in the **Major Physiological Disorders** section in chapter 3).

Harvest maturity is perhaps the most important preharvest factor influencing postharvest apple quality. Apple fruit can be harvested before they are fully ripe and will continue to ripen to good eating quality after harvest. Fruit that have developed to the stage where they can ripen to good quality after harvest are considered mature. Fruit that is harvested before it is mature is generally smaller and lacking in flavor, more subject to water loss and shrivel after harvest, and more susceptible to storage disorders such as bitter pit and scald. Fruit that is harvested overmature is softer, may have off flavors, is more susceptible to decay and storage breakdown, and generally has a shorter storage life.

The optimum harvest maturity differs for fruit destined for long-term storage in air or controlled atmospheres and fruit that will be marketed within a short period of time. Fruit destined for storage should be harvested before the fruit begins the period of rapid ripening (the climacteric), which is denoted by an increase in fruit respiration rates and ethylene production. Fruit harvested for immediate marketing can remain on the tree a week or two longer (depending on the climate) and may accumulate additional sugars for improved eating quality. However, harvesting of overmature fruit, even for immediate marketing, should be avoided as this results in soft fruit with low acidity levels and poor quality.

There are several fruit characteristics that can be monitored to determine advances in maturity on the tree (see table 4.1). These characteristics should be measured on 20 to 30 apples from at least five typical trees in the orchard. The most commonly monitored characteristics include starch content, firmness, and ground (non-red) color. Starch content can be measured by staining the center cross section of the apple with a starch iodine solution (see recipe below and color plate 4.1). The iodine solution turns starch black and allows an estimate to be made of fruit starch content. Starch charts can be used to determine a starch score based on the percentage of the cross section clear of staining (see color plate 4.2). Fruit firmness is determined by measuring the force required to puncture the apple flesh (skin removed) with a $\frac{7}{16}$-inch (11-mm) probe fitted to a penetrometer (see color plate 4.3).

For some apple varieties such as Gala and Fuji, ground color change from green to white to yellow is a good indicator of harvest maturity. The optimum values for each of these measurements should be determined for the variety of apple, the growing area, and the type of storage to be used. Rather than waiting to obtain the exact starch, firmness, and ground color, a change in one or more of these characteristics indicates the fruit is beginning to ripen. Testing of these characteristics should begin approximately 4 weeks before normal harvest so that changes can be detected. Many apple varieties grown in California are harvested two to three times due to the spread of

maturity on the tree. Visible indicators of maturity, such as ground color, are necessary to guide harvesters in multiple-pick situations.

Starch Iodine Solution
(0.1% iodine, 1% potassium iodide)

Dissolve 1 teaspoon (10 grams) of potassium iodide crystals in 1⅛ cup of clean water in a 1-quart container.

Gently swirl until the crystals dissolve.

Add ¼ teaspoon (2.5 grams) iodine and swirl until iodine dissolves (this may take a while).

Dilute this solution with clean water to make 1 quart.

The solution is sensitive to light and should be stored in a dark container or wrapped in aluminum foil. Fresh solution should be made each season. These chemicals are available at most drug stores.

HARVESTING AND PACKING

Careful handling of organic fruit to avoid injuries maintains fruit quality and reduces attack by disease-

Table 4.1. General guidelines for harvest maturity of some apple cultivars.

	Firmness (lbs-force)	Starch score (see color plate 4.2)	Ground color
Red Delicious			
Storage	17–18	2–3	light green or white
Immediate market	16	4	white
Golden Delicious			
Storage	16–17	2–3	greenish-white
Immediate market	15	4	yellow-green
Fuji			
Storage	16–17	4–5	light green
Immediate market	15	5–6	light green to white
Gala			
Storage	17–18	1–2	light green
Immediate market	15	3–4	light yellow to white
Granny Smith			
Storage	16–17	2–3*	not applicable
Immediate market	15–16	4–5	not applicable

*A minimum average starch score of 2.5 for 30 apples per orchard, collected from representative trees, is required in California.

causing organisms. Sanitation in the orchard and packing area also reduces the potential for fruit contamination. Diseased fruit should be kept out of the harvest bin whenever possible; it should either be turned back into the soil or removed from the orchard.

A physical separation between initial fruit sorting areas and the rest of the packing facility can reduce the spore load in the packing house. Diseased fruit sorted out during the packing operation should be moved to an area away from the packing shed to prevent spore spread to healthy fruit.

Harvest and packinghouse procedures are detailed in *Commercial Apple Growing in California* (ANR Publication 2456, 1992). Consult your certifier regarding allowable chlorine levels in wash water ("dump water").

··

TEMPERATURE MANAGEMENT

Precooling

Cooling can be accomplished in one of three ways: room cooling, hydrocooling, or forced-air cooling. Room cooling is the slowest method of precooling. Pro-

viding high rates of air flow and leaving space between bins and along the walls for air circulation speeds cooling. Bins with vented sides cool more rapidly. Forced-air cooling provides more rapid cooling by forcing cold air past the fruit. Excessive water loss can occur if fruit remains on the forced-air cooler longer than necessary to reach just near the storage temperature. Hydrocooling can provide very rapid cooling of apples. Bins should have good bottom drainage. The disadvantage of hydrocooling is the use of water, which can spread disease organisms to healthy fruit before storage. Use of chlorine is allowed at drinking water standards, but this is insufficient for decay control.

Cold Storage

Most apple varieties grown organically in California should be stored at the lowest safe temperature that still avoids freezing. The freezing point is inversely related to the soluble solids content of the fruit; the higher the soluble solids content, the lower the freezing point. Air distribution patterns and the accuracy and range of thermostatic controls influence temperature variability.

The majority of apple varieties grown in California can be safely stored at 32°F (0°C) without danger of freezing. The exceptions include McIntosh and Yellow Newtown apples. To prevent injury, California Yellow Newtown and McIntosh apples must be stored at 40°F (4.4°C) and 35.6°F (2°C), respectively, even though Yellow Newtowns grown in other areas of the country can be stored at 32°F (0°C). While a temperature of 33°F (0.6°C) is often recommended for Granny Smith apples, many have been successfully stored at 32°F (0°C) in California.

A relative humidity of 90 to 95 percent is required to prevent water loss. The rate of loading warm fruit into the cold room should be adjusted to avoid exceeding available refrigeration capacity. Many factors must be considered in determining the loading rate of a cooler. For example, a typical plant operating at 60 percent efficiency should handle 2 tons (1.8 metric tons) of apples per day per ton (0.9 metric ton) of refrigeration. If loading consistently exceeds capacity, expansion of refrigeration capacity should be considered.

Low Storage Temperatures Reduce Ripening and Decay

Rapid cooling of apple fruit to near storage temperature is very important for several reasons. Low temperatures decrease the respiration rate of the fruit. As fruit respire, they use their carbohydrate reserves and give off carbon dioxide. The more the fruit respires, the shorter its storage life will be. Low temperatures also reduce the rate of ethylene production. Ethylene is a gas naturally produced by the fruit that stimulates the ripening process and promotes the development of storage scald. Rapidly cooling the fruit reduces the amount of ethylene produced, thereby maintaining low levels of the gas in storage and reducing fruit sensitivity to ethylene. Rapid cooling and maintenance of low storage temperatures are also the most effective ways to reduce the development and spread of decay. Growth of decay organisms is greatly slowed or stopped at low temperatures, depending on the species of fungus involved.

High Relative Humidity Reduces Water Loss and Shrivel

Apples should be stored at 80 to 95 percent relative humidity. The longer the storage, the greater the need for high relative humidity to prevent excessive fruit shrivel. The most satisfactory means of achieving high relative humidity is through proper design of storage refrigeration. Large cooling surfaces can be operated at desired room temperatures, causing less water condensation from room air. Heavy insulation and proper management of a storage room to minimize air warming also helps maintain a high relative humidity. Humidifiers that add water to the room air may be useful, but greater moisture condensation on the cooling surfaces will increase the defrost frequency of dry coil systems.

If wooden bins are used, wetting the bins after loading in the cooling room helps increase relative humidity by reducing water absorption by the bins. Plastic bins do not absorb water in storage.

Warm fruit loses water at a much higher rate than cold fruit, especially if the relative humidity in the air is less than 95 percent. Losses of water are losses in salable weight and can result in fruit shrivel and reduced fruit gloss. Water loss is cumulative from the time the fruit are harvested until consumption. Visible shrivel does not occur until a critical level of water is lost. Before the critical level is reached, there is no visible sign that water loss has occurred. Rapid transport of fruit from the field to the cooler, rapid cooling, and maintenance of 90 to 95 percent relative humidity in storage are essential to reduce fruit water loss. The use of plastic bin liners can reduce water loss in storage, particularly if relative humidity is less than 95 percent. The disadvantage of using plastic liners is a significant reduction in cooling rate.

CONTROLLED-ATMOSPHERE STORAGE

Controlled-atmosphere storage is used to extend the market life of apples. While originally used for storage of chilling-sensitive varieties (such as Yellow Newtown and McIntosh), it is now commonly used for all apple varieties. As a supplement to cold storage practices, controlled-atmosphere storage involves reducing the oxygen concentration and raising the carbon dioxide concentration of the storage atmosphere. Such manipulations slow the respiration rate of apples and decay organisms, thus slowing apple deterioration. Under controlled-atmosphere storage, apple fruit produce less ethylene and are less affected by it in the storage atmosphere. Fruit stored in a controlled atmosphere are often more firm, have greater retention of soluble solids and titratable acidity, and have less bitter pit compared with fruit from the same lot stored in regular cold storage. Very low oxygen atmospheres (0.5 to 1.0 percent) can also delay the onset of storage scald; however, each variety's tolerance at these low oxygen levels must be established for each maturity stage prior to large scale use of this technique.

Controlled-atmosphere storage rooms must be specially designed to

- be relatively gas-tight, even under changing atmospheric pressure conditions

- allow removal of excess carbon dioxide from the atmosphere

- allow the addition of air to maintain a minimum safe oxygen level

In modern facilities, the initial desired atmospheric concentrations are often established by nitrogen generators, which remove excess oxygen by nitrogen flushing. Carbon dioxide can be adjusted initially by nitrogen flushing, scrubbing with powdered lime, or absorption with an alkaline solution. Older systems burn off excess oxygen. Once the desired atmosphere is attained, the nitrogen generator can be used to remove excess carbon dioxide or to overcome problems (maintenance, gas leaks, and so on).

While apple fruit often benefit from storage under recommended controlled atmospheric conditions, they can be injured by storage at too low an oxygen concentration or too high a carbon dioxide concentration. Tolerance varies depending on the variety. Late harvested fruit of high maturity should not be stored in controlled-atmosphere storage. Good temperature management is as important in controlled-atmosphere storage as in regular air storage (see table 4.2).

The controlled-atmosphere environment will not support human life. Controlled-atmosphere storage rooms must be carefully posted and precautions taken to assure that people do not enter. Before people can safely enter, rooms must be completely ventilated to the outside. Entrance during storage must be with the use of approved life-support systems and with careful adherence to all legal requirements for work in such environments.

....

SANITATION DURING PROCESSING OF ORGANIC APPLES

The primary precautions of any processing unit are the sanitation of equipment and fruit prior to processing. Care must be taken to avoid contamination with any manure products in the orchard that would risk the introduction of bacteria into the food chain.

Another important consideration is the removal of those apples or parts of apples that have been infected with codling moth. Codling moth–damaged fruit has been associated with certain fungi that enter wounds created by the codling moth larvae and break down the fruit. In the breakdown process, the fungi can create toxins called aflotoxins that are dangerous even in very small amounts.

If fruit is being cut in any way, it must be prepared in a certified facility that is periodically inspected by the California Department of Health Services. Processing fruit should be washed in a disinfectant solution that is approved by a certification agency. Fruit should be carefully inspected and if codling moth damage is present, it should be cut to remove any blemished flesh. Tables, equipment, blades, or anything that comes in contact with the cut fruit should be periodically sterilized with acceptable disinfectants. There are specific time and temperature requirements for proper and safe heat pasteurization. Research is now being conducted on different methods of disinfecting apple juice with ozone and ultraviolet light to retain freshness without heat pasteurization and loss of flavor.

Table 4.2. Controlled atmosphere and temperature recommendations for storage of California apples.

Cultivar	Percent O_2	Percent CO_2	Temperature °F (°C)	Maximum storage (months)	Comments
Red Delicious	1.5–2.5	1–3	31–34 (-0.5–1)	8–10	CO_2 injury potential
Golden Delicious	1–2	1.5–2.5	31–34(-0.5–1)	8–10	—
Granny Smith	1–2	1–1.2	32–34 (0–1)	8–10	—
Fuji	1–2.5	0.5–1	32–34 (0–1)	7–8	CO_2 injury potential
Gala	1–2	1–2	31–34 (-0.5–1)	5–6	Rapid cooling and controlled atmosphere
Yellow Newtown	3	5–8	35–40 (2–4.5)	2–4	—

5

Marketing Considerations

Commodities that are produced organically are typically sold for a higher price than conventionally grown products. Price premiums for fresh-market organic apples have ranged from 20 to nearly 100 percent the price of conventional apples, depending on variety and changes in supply conditions. For example, if growers are early to market, returns may be higher due to limited market competition and heightened consumer demand. Also, growers with good quality produce and consistent supply are generally better able to market their product effectively on a year-to-year basis. Alternatively, imports and large crops may cause market gluts, negatively impacting grower returns.

Market conditions for 1998 were reportedly adverse for the organic market, at least for growers, because of two significant factors. International demand for Washington's massive apple supply declined markedly due to decreased demand in economically depressed Asian markets. Concurrently, China's huge acreage of apple plantings is beginning to affect global supply and depress prices. The consequent market impact is that Washington apples are being marketed in the United States at historically low prices—reportedly as low as $4 per box of wholesale conventional apples—pulling down U.S. prices for conventional as well as organic apples. Premiums to growers also vary depending on the marketing channel utilized.

Like their conventional counterparts, organic producers need to take into account market risks as well as production risks since they cannot depend on price or yield stability. Instead of using the most recent price as a market indicator, growers may need to average prices over the past several years to get a better indication of market potential, while also considering long-term trends in acreage and potential changes in supply.

QUALITY

If organic commodities are to continue to command a premium price, quality must reflect that price. Consumers tend to view quality as a combination of attributes such as appearance, flavor, color, and freshness. In general, to increase the sales of organically produced apples, producers and marketers need to focus on the four Ps of marketing: product, place, promotion, and price. With respect to product, quality is key.

Organically grown apples must meet the same minimum quality grades and standards as conventionally grown apples. While growers, marketers, and consumers may have different perceptions of quality, the appearance of fresh market commodities probably impacts grower returns more significantly than all other quality factors. For example, fruit that is russeted, blemished, or distorted is not often tolerated by today's consumers or by current grades and standards. Fruit size and color also impact grower returns; larger, well-colored fruit often command a higher market price. These are visual characteristics that are generally preferred by marketers and consumers although they are not necessarily correlated with better overall nutritional value, flavor, or food safety. But flavor, texture, and freshness do affect repeat purchases.

The importance of color in apple marketing cannot be overstated. Even in green varieties like Granny Smith, a deep green color and sour taste are usually preferred by the majority of green apple buyers. This is evident even though Granny Smith becomes much sweeter and somewhat yellow-green in color when fully ripe. Some growers do, however, sell these fully ripe apples in niche markets as late-harvest Granny Smiths to appeal to a segment of organic apple consumers.

Fuji is another example of a variety that sells very well as a yellow-orange fruit as long as it is the only apple on the market at the time. However, as soon as full red-colored fruit becomes available in volume, the price for yellow-orange fruit drops dramatically. This is one of the historical reasons why red varieties have not been grown in areas where they cannot achieve the most preferred color.

When mature, the original Red Delicious has a yellow background color attractively overlaid with red stripes. Since the 1920s when the first sport mutations (sub or color varieties) were discovered, several hundred new full-colored red sports have been introduced. Along with the improved red color comes earlier coloring, so the fruit appears ready for harvest long before it is actually mature. When mature, it turns a more dull purple-red color. Consequently, there is a strong tendency to pick Red Delicious sports well in advance of optimum edible maturity. Such fruit usually depresses the market and makes it difficult to move mature fruit when it becomes available.

Although fresh-market apples are a perishable product, they can be held in cold storage for an extended period of time to maintain quality. This is an advantage to the grower if the product cannot be sold immediately or if current market prices are low. But unless prices are anticipated to increase later in the year, apples should be sold in an expedient manner for growers to derive the most satisfactory returns.

....

DEMAND

Apple producers and marketers need to study their markets—the demographic profile of their customers and their preferences. A proportion of consumers prefer organic fruit and are willing to pay more for it. Promotional information should inform these consumers about organic products, and the products should be priced to appeal to them.

Demographics

According to a recent study (Jolly 1996) regarding the demographic characteristics of organic food purchasers, more buyers were in service and white-collar occupations as compared with blue-collar occupations. They also tended to live in smaller towns and cities or the largest urban centers. Education and income were not statistically significant factors in identifying organic food buyers although surveys have generally shown that more organic products are purchased by consumers with annual income levels of $12,000 to

$22,400, and above $35,000. The study showed that organic produce shoppers tended to be younger—the age cohorts 18 to 29 and 40 to 49 had the highest levels of consumers.

Cities with a high proportion of young people in education or white-collar occupations would likely offer strong markets for organically produced apples. These towns or areas of cities tend to support cultures that are experimental and dynamic—college towns, cities with a strong high-tech industry, sunbelt cities, and cultural incubators such as San Francisco, Los Angeles, Berkeley, New York, Boston, and Madison, Wisconsin.

Consumer Preferences and Price Responsiveness

A consumer survey conducted in Marin, Sacramento, and San Diego counties in 1987 (Jolly et al. 1989) found strong expressed consumer preferences for organically produced products. Organic foods were identified with the following perceived attributes, from highest to lowest frequencies: safety, freshness, general health benefits, nutritional value, effect on the environment, flavor, and general appearance. Thus, the perceptions of organic foods position them favorably in the marketplace.

Further indication of the perceptions of organic products compared with their conventional counterparts is provided by responses to the question as to whether organic foods are "better," "worse," or "about the same" as conventional foods. Approximately 57 percent of the respondents perceived organic foods as better, 35 percent as about the same, and only 7 percent as worse. While the proportions may have shifted somewhat since this survey, there is no indication that they have become more adverse for organic products. Still, producers should understand that the market is essentially still a niche market and will likely remain so for several years. This has to do with the factors of supply and demand. Only 18 percent of the survey respondents reported purchasing organic products 5 to 30 times per month. Another 37 percent purchased organic products from 1 to 4.3 times per month. Forty-five percent of respondents reported purchasing organic products only rarely.

Major supply-side constraints identified by consumers included price differentials for organic foods, locations of stores that carry organic products, and time to search for organic products. (See table 5.1.)

On the demand side, consumer willingness to pay price differentials and to absorb the opportunity cost of time spent finding the product are potentially significant constraints. Comparing the market prices of conventional and organic apples, Thompson and Kidwell (1998) found the following prices as shown in table 5.2.

In this survey, the average price differential was 43 percent. At this level of price differential the market niche for organic apples is potentially significant. The consumer survey by Jolly et al. (1989) found that 41 percent of that study's consumer respondents were willing to pay a price differential of 44 percent on a conventional base price of 68 cents. (See table 5.3.)

Note, however, that when retail price premiums for organic products rise to 74 percent above conventional prices, potential buyers decline from 41 percent to a mere 8 percent. Therefore, there is a tradeoff between price differential and volume. This puts some pressure on growers to keep yields high and quality good in order to avoid relying too heavily on price differentials for revenues and depend more on a combination of yield, quality, and price premiums.

Table 5.1. Constraints identified by consumers who have not continued purchasing organic foods.

Item	Percent of respondents
High price	56.9
Location of store(s)	53.5
Time to search (for stores and products)	47.1
Appearance	6.8
Flavor	5.8
Color	5.8
Quality	5.3
Don't know	8.9
Other	16.2

Source: Jolly et al. 1989.

Table 5.2. Apple price comparisons.

	Conventional ($/lb)	Organic ($/lb)
Average price	1.04	1.49
Minimum price	0.79	0.99
Maximum price	1.39	1.99

Source: Thompson and Kidwell 1998.

Table 5.3. Willingness to purchase organic apples at alternative prices (n = 337).

Conventional price ($/lb)	Organic price ($/lb)	Price differential (%)	Percent of all respondents
0.68	0.78	14.71	45.4
0.68	0.98	44.12	41.1
0.68	1.18	73.53	8.2
0.68	1.28	88.24	2.3
0.68	1.68	147.06	3.1
0.68	0.98	37.00*	

*Weighted average price differential.
Source: Jolly 1989.

MARKETING CHANNELS

Returns to growers vary with the type of marketing channel utilized. For some producers it may be more expedient to use the services of a marketing intermediary. Where resources are favorable, direct marketing may provide viable and more profitable options. There are definite advantages and disadvantages to each option.

Intermediaries

Apples that are grown organically for the fresh market are often custom-packed after harvest and sold through a sales agent or local produce broker. Sales agents charge a fee or commission for connecting growers and buyers. When growers use a sales agent, they often enlist the services of a consolidator to cool, inventory, and ship their product. Sales agents' fees are generally 9 to 10 percent of gross sales, while consolidators charge a flat fee per box.

Alternatively, produce brokers act as intermediaries between producers and buyers. They receive the product after packing and facilitate cooling, handling, sales, and distribution for a fee or commission. For apples, produce brokers' fees range from 10 to 12 percent of the gross sales. A produce broker's commission customarily excludes cooling fees. Sale of the product is generally guaranteed by the produce broker based on buyer acceptance.

Some producers have made special arrangements with certain supermarkets or chain stores to provide a specific product type at a specific time for a negotiated price. The buyer usually has some input into the quality of the product and helps promote the item. Smaller markets usually require direct delivery, but in the process the grower develops relationships with produce managers that generally foster future sales and better prices.

Direct Sales to Consumers

Where feasible, direct selling to consumers can provide lucrative marketing alternatives. There is a range of alternatives, from farmers' markets to roadside stands.

Farmers' Markets. Farmers' markets are an excellent outlet for organic apples, especially if the fruit are attractive and flavorful. Prices at farmers' markets are comparable to retail at specialty markets. Farmers' markets are excellent places to meet customers, try new sales ideas, develop confidence in your product, learn how to merchandise, and receive immediate consumer feedback. However, growers should be aware that direct marketing requires much travel, time, and labor, and farmers' markets sales do not typically exceed 20 to 50 boxes per event. (California's farmers' markets are listed on the Internet at http://farmersmarket. ucdavis.edu/)

Gaining access to farmers' markets is increasingly difficult; in some cases there are waiting lists for farmers. But fortunate growers find lucrative markets for fresh produce as well as for juices and other processed products. Farmers' markets are viewed positively by urban consumers and are gaining in popularity.

Data from a California survey conducted in San Diego County in 1998 (Lobo et al.) confirm the trend toward strong consumer preferences for direct markets. Table 5.4 shows the attributes associated with farmers' markets. The top four attributes identified with farmers' markets were "freshness," "quality," "taste," and "help local farmers/locally grown." Approximately equal proportions of the sample (about one-third) perceived prices to be higher or lower than supermarket prices. However, 73 percent perceived quality to be superior to supermarket produce, a surprising response given the proximity of California's supermarkets to production areas. Two-thirds of the respondents preferred products to have a locally grown label and half indicated a willingness to pay more for locally grown products.

As with any marketing effort, sellers at farmers' markets should emphasize presentation (appearance), quality, and price. The consumer needs to perceive value and is generally willing to pay for attributes such as locally grown, fresh, superior flavor, and organic. Repeat business is the key to success so attention must be given to positive customer relations.

Community Supported Agriculture (CSA). Community supported agriculture, sometimes known as consumer supported agriculture or subscription agriculture, is another form of direct marketing that has developed as an alternative marketing arrangement amenable to family-scale farming. It lends itself to operations that are somewhat easily accessible to an urban area, to situations in which entrepreneurial and marketing talent and knowledge are available, and labor and management are not severely constrained.

Ideally, in community supported agriculture the consumer participates in the operation of the farm, advancing cash, and investing labor for the production of the crop. More realistically, consumers pay a specified amount in advance for weekly or biweekly deliveries of boxes of produce. Diversity is required to somewhat mimic the choices that consumers might make if they were shopping in a supermarket. Thus, one of the innovations that was developed to make CSA work is cooperation between farms with different kinds of products. Apple growers might need to link with other produce growers by offering to supply one or more CSA groups with apples. Even then, providing different varieties might be an asset. CSAs and subscription farm sales require a big investment in time and promotion to develop the customer base and to deliver the product at regular intervals. The main advantages to CSA are guaranteed payment and up-front funds to finance some of the farming expenses. As with farmers' markets and other direct sales methods, increased returns and improved cash flow are also potential benefits.

Roadside Farm Stands. Roadside farm stands should not be overlooked as potential outlets for organically produced apples and processed product sales. Product safety measures should be taken to reduce the risks of bacterial contamination. Growers should research and follow the best practices for product safety. The University of California Cooperative Extension and the land-grant universities are good sources for product safety information. Other potential sources are health departments and agricultural commissioner offices.

Table 5.4. Factors favoring patronage of San Diego's farmers' markets.*

	Percent of respondents[†]
Freshness	92
Quality	87
Taste	76
Locally grown product	71
Help local farmers	71
Nutritional value	48
Atmosphere	46
Best value for money	41
Convenience	38
Price	36
Know grower	14
Other	8

*Consumers could choose multiple responses.
[†]Rounded to nearest 1 percent.
Source: Lobo et al. 1998.

MARKET PERFORMANCE

Absent isolated events, the performance of organic markets are partially determined by supply and demand conditions in the conventional market. Since yields are, in general, lower in organic systems, price differentials are key to economic performance. Large gluts in the conventional market can depress conventional prices, leading to an exaggeration of the price differential between conventional and organic. This would lead to an adverse consumer response and a consequent decrease in organic prices.

Thus, as growers make decisions about investments in organic acreage, they need to acquire relevant information on production practices to maximize the output of high quality organic apples at reasonable costs. They also need to examine trends in acreage and plantings for conventional and organic apples. Since the apple market is increasingly a global one, the grower's assessment of potential market scenarios needs to examine global trends in production. However, this kind of analysis might invite more caution than necessary. Where market outlets are more local and direct, market analysis can be more geographically circumscribed. Recent market outcomes illustrate the interdependence of the organic and conventional markets.

The data in table 5.5 indicate the volatility of the organic apple market, reflecting changes in the U.S. and global supplies of fresh and processing apples. Growers must be aware of production and market risks when they make investment decisions. The following chapter on economic performance provides a frame-work growers can use to make decisions about organic production and to monitor the performance of their orchards. Actual outcomes will vary from operation to operation depending on location, soils, varieties, pest pressures, and so on.

Table 5.5. Prices for selected organic apples in California.

Grade	1997 Price ($)	1998 Price ($)
Juicers	200/ton	100 and less/ton
Peelers		
2–2	280/ton	150/ton
2 and over	300/ton	150/ton
Fresh-market early Gravensteins and Galas		
88s* and 100s	38/box	34/box
113s	34/box	30/box
125s	30/box	26/box
Bags	18–20/box	not available
Lates		
88s and 100s	30/box	22/box
113s	26/box	18/box
125s	18/box	10/box

*Number of apples per 40-pound box.
Source: Kozlowski 1999.

6

Economic Performance

Conversion to certified organic techniques can involve cost and risk. However, organic apples can be highly profitable in well-managed, high-yielding (10 to 20 tons/acre [22.4 to 44.8 metric ton/ha]), fresh-market orchards. Price premiums for organic apples are currently an important stimulus to conversion and certification, but it is difficult to predict the stability of these premiums, especially if the supply of organic apples increases at a higher rate than demand. Although no numbers are currently available for the size of the organic apple market specifically, we do know that the sales of all organic commodities in California represent less than 1 percent of total farm sales, and organic fruits and nuts represent roughly one-third of all organic sales. By inference, the market for organic apples is still small.

Given fluctuations in net returns in some cases, it is important that organic apple production decisions be made with full knowledge of local technical and marketing conditions. If reliable organic pest, soil, and tree management systems can be devised for a given site, a transition management plan should be implemented and should be continually evaluated, updated, and compared to conventional practices and yields.

YIELD

Yields for organic apples vary depending on a number of factors including orchard age, planting density, apple variety, production location, irrigation practices, and yearly growing conditions. Apples specifically earmarked for the fresh market are required to meet certain grades and standards. The portion of the crop that does not meet fresh-market standards is culled for processing. Apple yields are expressed as (1) gross tonnage per acre, (2) percent of total tonnage taken to the packinghouse with fresh-market potential, and (3) pack-out, or the portion of the crop that is determined saleable fresh-market fruit.

Pack-out is expressed in terms of percentage of gross tonnage and also in terms of boxes. Boxes are packed in one of three ways: cello-bagged, loose-packed, or tray-packed. Apple size determines the method of packing. For example, small-sized apples are generally cello-bagged, and large-sized apples are tray-packed. However, in some cases special orders may dictate a different packing protocol. Table 6.1 shows estimated pack-out ranges for Central and North Coast fresh-market organic apples.

On the Central Coast, yields for organically produced apples range from 7 (low-density plantings) to 30 (high-density plantings) gross tons per acre. An estimated 70 to 95 percent of this tonnage goes to the packing shed; some of this fruit is then culled for processing. In the North Coast region, yields range from 7 (low-density plantings) to 25 (high-density plantings) gross tons per acre. An estimated 70 to 85 percent of this tonnage goes to the packing shed; some of this fruit is then culled for processing. Depending on the operation's size, packing is done by a custom packinghouse or by the grower.

AN EXAMPLE: ESTIMATED COSTS AND EXPECTED RETURNS FOR CENTRAL COAST ORGANIC APPLES

A number of basic economic tools can be used to analyze business decisions for an organic apple-farming operation. These include (1) whole farm budgets, (2) enterprise budgets, (3) partial budgets, and (4) capital budgets. The type of budget used in an analysis depends on the needs of each apple grower or farm manager. Whole farm budgets are appropriately used when an entire business is to be evaluated. Enterprise budgets are useful for determining the potential profitability of a specific commodity. Partial budgets enable growers and managers to examine the financial impact of specific changes within a cropping system, for example, changing pest management techniques or practices. Capital budgets are used to assess the impact of long-term business changes such as the purchase of land or equipment.

An enterprise budget for 1994, including a monthly cash flow statement, for a mature organic apple operation on the Central Coast is presented in tables 6.2 to 6.4. Costs are based on representative cultural practices; these practices are not used every year or by all growers. While production practices have not significantly changed since the cost and returns study presented was completed in 1994 (Klonsky et al.), keep in mind that several costs have increased. In particular, labor rates and interest rates have increased in the last few years.

The following are the underlying assumptions used to derive the cost and return estimate.

Table 6.1. Approximate pack-out yield ranges for Californian fresh-market organic apples.*

Apple variety	Boxes[†] per acre	Percent of gross tonnage
Central Coast		
Granny Smith	355–600	50–60
Jonagold[‡]	700	70
McIntosh	225–300	45–80
Yellow Newtown Pippin	120–240	25–30
North Coast		
Golden Delicious	190–550	50–55
Gravenstein	315–385	42–51
Jonathan	315–425	42–50
McIntosh	170–300	45–60
Red Rome	225–625	52–63

*Tree spacing is 12 by 18 feet for a total of 202 trees per acre.
[†]Boxes hold 40 pounds (18 kg).
[‡]Jonagold yield is for a high-density planting. No ranges are given.

• Orchard Size: The total orchard size is 40 acres (16 ha). Land is assumed to be owned by the grower and is valued at $15,000 per acre. This cost is within a range of values for orchard land on the Central Coast. Land is not depreciated.

• Orchard Establishment: The establishment cost is the sum of the costs for the land preparation, trees, planting, cash overhead, and production expenses for growing the trees through the first year that apples are harvested (year 5). The establishment cost is used to determine the noncash overhead expenses, depreciation, and interest on investment during the production years. The orchard life is assumed to be 25 years beyond the 5 establishment years.

• Variety and Spacing: The apple varieties (for production and cross-pollination) are not specified. Factors affecting varietal selection include adaptability to climatic region, time to maturity, and marketability. Trees are planted with a spacing of 12 feet by 18 feet (3.7 m by 5.5 m) and 202 trees per acre.

• Yield: The assumed gross yield is 13 tons per acre (29 metric ton/ha). The assumed fresh-market yield is 7.5 tons or 375 boxes per acre (17 metric ton/ha) representing a 58 percent pack-out. Boxes weigh 40 pounds (18 kg) and are tray-packed. In addition, 5.5 tons (5 metric tons) are assumed to be sold to a processor for the organic market. These yields fall within the range of yields received by growers in this area.

• Labor: Basic hourly wages for workers are $6.60 and $5.45 for machine operators and fieldworkers, respectively. Adding 34 percent for workers compensation, social security, and other benefits increases the labor rates to $8.85 per hour for machine labor and $7.30 per hour for manual labor. The labor hours for operations involving machinery are 20 percent higher than actual operation time due to the extra time involved in equipment setup, moving, maintenance, and repair.

• Interest on Operating Capital: This interest rate is based on cash cultural costs. It is calculated monthly until harvest at the rate of 7.89 percent per year. This interest can be viewed as the cost of a production loan. For a business that is self-financed, the interest can be seen as the opportunity cost of tying up capital in the crop.

Tables 6.2, 6.3, and 6.4 provide information for the same orchard and set of assumptions. Each table presents the information in a different format and as such contains different levels of detail on production practices, inputs, and costs.

Table 6.2 lists the cash and labor costs by cultural operation. The operations are listed in order of occurrence and the cost of the material inputs are listed. Cash and noncash overhead costs are included to calculate total costs of production excluding management and risk. Table 6.3 details the operating costs according to the inputs described by operation in table 6.2. The total quantities and costs per unit of each input are presented. The cash and noncash overhead costs are not included to avoid redundancy with table 6.2. Table 6.4 lists the total operating costs by operation from table 6.2 on a monthly basis. The total cash costs per month are included.

For the hypothetical orchard presented, the total cash costs are $5,711 per acre at a yield of 375 forty-pound tray-packed boxes for fresh-market apples and 5.5 tons (5 metric tons) of processing apples. The total costs including depreciation and interest on buildings, land, orchard establishment, equipment, and irrigation system are $7,240 per acre.

For product marketed as organic, returns to growers range from $12 to $27 per 40-pound tray-packed box for fresh-market and $150 to $260 per ton for processing apples. For prices at or below $15.50 per box or yields below 475 boxes per acre, it is not profitable to produce organic apples. At a high price of $27 per box the break-even yield is 221 boxes per acre. Actual economic performance will depend on numerous factors including variety, site conditions, yearly production conditions, and out-of-state and foreign imports.

Table 6.2. 1994 operation costs for fresh-market organic apples on the Central Coast.

Operation	Operation time (hr/acre)	Labor ($/acre)	Fuel and repairs ($/acre)	Material ($/acre)	Custom/rent ($/acre)	Total cost ($/acre)
Cultural costs						
Disc 2X, ground preparation	0.86	9	6	—	—	15
Plant cover crop, broadcast seed	0.33	7	2	42	—	51
Disc, cover seed	0.43	5	3	—	—	8
Prune orchard	45.00	328	—	—	—	328
Oil spray 2X	0.50	5	4	39	—	48
Pruning disposal	1.30	23	7	0	—	30
Tree replacement, 3 per acre	1.00	11	5	19	—	35
Irrigate and prune replants	2.00	14	—	5	—	19
Lime sulfur application 2X	0.50	5	4	48	—	57
Pollination	0.00	—	—	—	32	32
Mow cover crop	0.33	4	2	—	—	6
Tie/hang pheromones, April	3.00	22	—	118	—	140
Wettable sulfur application 3X	0.75	8	6	3	—	17
Disc, incorp. cover crop	0.43	5	3	—	—	8
Spread composted manure	3.00	32	19	75	—	126
Disc, incorp. cover crop and compost	0.43	5	3	—	—	8
Hand weed 2X	20.00	146	—	—	—	146
Snail removal, ½ of acreage	5.00	36	—	—	—	36
Hand thin	40.00	292	—	—	—	292
Tie/hang pheromones, June	3.00	22	—	59	—	81
Disc 2X, weed control/surface prep.	0.86	9	6	—	—	15
Irrigation 3X	2.55	19	—	56	—	75
Insecticidal soap, ⅓ of acreage	0.08	1	1	6	—	8
Prop trees	7.00	51	—	—	—	51
Broken limbs, miscellaneous care	0.10	1	—	—	—	1
Rodent control, trap	2.00	15	—	—	—	15
Pickup truck use	7.17	76	46	—	—	122
Total cultural costs	147.62	1,151	117	470	32	1,770
Harvest costs						
Hand harvest	82.00	599	—	—	—	599
Equipment use	0.40	4	2	—	—	6
Transport to packing shed	4.00	42	29	—	—	71
Packing services	0.00	—	—	401	1,875	2,276
Consolidation services	0.00	—	—	—	263	263
Total harvest costs	86.40	645	31	401	2,138	3,215

Table 6.2. Continued.

Operation	Operation time (hr/acre)	Labor ($/acre)	Fuel and repairs ($/acre)	Material ($/acre)	Custom/rent ($/acre)	Total cost ($/acre)
Assessment costs						
CDFAOP registration fees	—	—	—	11	—	11
CCOF membership fees	—	—	—	3	—	3
CCOF inspection fees	—	—	—	2	—	2
CCOF .5% of gross sales	—	—	—	38	—	38
Total assessment costs	—	—	—	54	—	54
Interest on operating capital @ 7.89%	102					
Total operating costs/acre		1,796	148	925	2,170	5,141
Cash overhead costs						
Office expense						250
Tissue/soil analysis						4
Sanitation services						16
Liability insurance						8
Property taxes						111
Property insurance						158
Investment repairs						23
Total cash overhead costs						570
Total cash costs/acre						5,711

Noncash overhead costs		Annual cost ($/producing acre)		
Investment	$/producing acre	Depreciation	Interest @ 3.72%	Total
Building	500	15	10	25
Fuel tanks and pumps	203	9	4	13
Shop tools	275	17	6	23
Land	15,000	—	558	558
Orchard establishment	9,428	377	175	552
Product bins	228	20	5	25
Irrigation pipe	162	14	3	17
Tree props	505	20	9	29
Pruning equipment	30	3	1	4
Harvest equipment	34	3	1	4
Irrigation system	440	16	9	25
ATV	190	34	4	38
Equipment	1,945	176	40	216
Total noncash overhead costs	28,940	704	825	1,529
Total costs/acre				7,240

Table 6.3. 1994 detail of input costs ($/acre) for fresh-market organic apples on the Central Coast.

Operating cost	Quantity/acre	Unit	Price or cost/unit	cost/acre
Cover crop seed				
Oats	50	pound	0.26	13
Bell beans	30	pound	0.39	12
Purple vetch	20	pound	0.86	17
Fertilizing materials				
Composted manure	4	ton	18.75	75
Pest management				
Horticultural oil	9	gallon	4.29	39
Lime sulfur	10	gallon	4.83	48
Wettable sulfur	12	pound	0.26	3
April pheromones	1	acre	117.98	118
June pheromones	1	acre	58.99	59
Insecticidal soap	.33	gallon	18.88	6
Tree replants				
Replace tree	3	acre	5.36	16
Carton tree	3	acre	1.00	3
Water				
Pumped	13	acre-inch	4.69	61
Custom				
Pollination	1	hive	32.00	32
Packing services	375	box	5.00	1,875
Consolidation fees	375	box	0.70	263
Packing materials				
Apple box	375	box	1.07	401
Assessments				
CDFAOP registration fees	1 acre		11.25	11
CCOF membership fees	1 acre		3.13	3
CCOF inspection fees	1 acre		2.50	2
CCOF .5% of gross sales	1acre		37.50	38
Labor (machine)	27 hr		8.85	240
Labor (nonmachine)	213 hr		7.30	1,555
Fuel, gas	18 gal		1.17	21
Fuel, diesel	47 gal		0.85	40
Lube	—	—	—	9
Machinery repair	—	—	—	79
Interest on operating capital @ 7.89%	—	—	—	102
Total operating costs/acre				5,141

Table 6.4. 1994 monthly cash costs per acre to produce organic fresh-market apples on the Central Coast.

Beginning Nov 1993 Ending Oct 1994	Nov 93	Dec 93	Jan 94	Feb 94	Mar 94	Apr 94	May 94	Jun 94	Jul 94	Aug 94	Sep 94	Oct 94	Total
Cultural													
Disc 2X, ground preparation	15	—	—	—	—	—	—	—	—	—	—	—	15
Plant cover crop, broadcast	51	—	—	—	—	—	—	—	—	—	—	—	51
Disc, cover seed	8	—	—	—	—	—	—	—	—	—	—	—	8
Prune orchard	—	110	109	109	—	—	—	—	—	—	—	—	328
Oil spray 2X	—	—	26	—	22	—	—	—	—	—	—	—	48
Pruning disposal	—	—	—	30	—	—	—	—	—	—	—	—	30
Tree replacement, 3 per acre	—	—	—	35	—	—	—	—	—	—	—	—	35
Irrigate and prune replants	—	—	—	19	—	—	—	—	—	—	—	—	19
Lime sulfur appl. 2X	—	—	—	—	29	28	—	—	—	—	—	—	57
Pollination	—	—	—	—	32	—	—	—	—	—	—	—	32
Mow cover crop	—	—	—	—	—	6	—	—	—	—	—	—	6
Tie/hang pheromones, April	—	—	—	—	—	140	—	—	—	—	—	—	140
Wettable sulfur appl. 3X	—	—	—	—	—	6	11	—	—	—	—	—	17
Disc, incorp. cover crop	—	—	—	—	—	8	—	—	—	—	—	—	8
Spread composted manure	—	—	—	—	—	126	—	—	—	—	—	—	126
Disc, incorp. cc and compost	—	—	—	—	—	8	—	—	—	—	—	—	8
Hand weed 2X	—	—	—	—	—	73	—	73	—	—	—	—	146
Snail removal ½ of acreage	—	—	—	—	—	—	36	—	—	—	—	—	36
Hand thin	—	—	—	—	—	—	146	146	—	—	—	—	292
Tie/hang pheromones, June	—	—	—	—	—	—	—	81	—	—	—	—	81
Disc 2X, weeds/surface prep.	—	—	—	—	—	—	—	8	7	—	—	—	15
Irrigation 3X	—	—	—	—	—	—	—	25	25	25	—	—	75
Insect. soap ⅓ of acreage	—	—	—	—	—	—	—	8	—	—	—	—	8
Prop trees	—	—	—	—	—	—	—	—	51	—	—	—	51
Broken limbs, misc. care	—	—	—	—	—	—	—	—	1	—	—	—	1
Rodent control, trap	—	—	—	—	—	—	—	—	—	15	—	—	15
Pickup truck use	—	—	—	—	—	—	—	—	—	—	122	—	122
Total cultural costs	74	110	135	193	83	395	193	341	84	40	122	—	1,770
Harvest													
Hand harvest	—	—	—	—	—	—	—	—	—	—	—	599	599
Equipment use	—	—	—	—	—	—	—	—	—	—	—	6	6
Transport to packing shed	—	—	—	—	—	—	—	—	—	—	—	71	71
Packing services	—	—	—	—	—	—	—	—	—	—	—	2,276	2,276
Consolidation services	—	—	—	—	—	—	—	—	—	—	—	263	263
Total harvest costs	—	—	—	—	—	—	—	—	—	—	—	3,215	3,215
Assessments													
CDFAOP registration fees	—	—	—	—	—	—	—	—	—	—	—	11	11
CCOF membership fees	—	—	—	—	—	—	—	—	—	—	—	3	3
CCOF inspection fees	—	—	—	—	—	—	—	—	—	—	—	2	2
CCOF .5% of gross sales	—	—	—	—	—	—	—	—	—	—	—	38	38
Total assessment costs	—	—	—	—	—	—	—	—	—	—	—	54	54
Interest on operating capital	—	1	2	3	4	7	8	10	11	11	12	33	102
Total operating costs/acre	74	111	137	196	87	402	201	351	95	51	134	3,302	5,141
Cash overhead													
Office expense	21	21	21	21	21	20	21	21	21	20	21	21	250
Tissue/soil analysis	—	—	—	—	—	—	—	—	—	—	—	4	4
Sanitation services	—	—	—	—	—	—	—	—	—	—	—	16	16
Liability insurance	—	—	—	—	—	—	—	—	—	—	—	8	8
Property taxes	—	55	—	—	—	56	—	—	—	—	—	—	111
Property insurance	—	—	158	—	—	—	—	—	—	—	—	—	158
Investment repairs	2	2	2	2	2	2	2	2	2	2	2	1	23
Total cash overhead costs	23	78	181	23	23	78	23	23	23	22	23	50	570
Total cash costs/acre	97	189	318	219	110	480	224	374	118	73	157	3,352	5,711

Orchard Management

Plate 2.1
Freedom apple variety

Plate 2.2
Goldrush apple variety

Plate 2.3
Liberty apple variety

Plate 2.4
Priscilla apple variety

Plate 2.5
William's Pride apple variety

Plate 2.6
Mowing a bell bean cover crop prior to disking. Incorporation of a legume cover crop can help satisfy the nutrient needs of an orchard.

Plate 2.7
Apples at ½-inch to 1-inch thinning stage 30 days after full bloom. Fruit must be thinned 30 to 45 days after full bloom in order to ensure adequate bloom for the following year's crop.

Plate 2.8
Fabric mulch is placed under apple trees to suppress weed growth.

Orchard Management

Plate 2.9
Drilled bell bean cover crop in an organic orchard. Legume and legume-grass blends are used to supply the soil with nitrogen and biomass.

Plate 2.10
Cover crops can be weighed in the orchard to determine how many pounds of nitrogen input they provide. (See **How to Calculate Nitrogen Input from a Cover Crop** on page 16.)

Plate 2.11
Grasses shown from left to right are zorro fescue, foxtail barley, annual ryegrass, blando brome, and wild oats. Note that the zorro fescue and blando brome are mature while the annual ryegrass is just flowering and still green.

3.1

3.2

3.3

3.4

3.5

3.6

3.7

3.8

Disease and Pest Management

Plate 3.1
Apple scab infection leads to blemishes on fruit.

Plate 3.2
Apple scab can cause blossom drop and fruit loss.

Plate 3.3
Russeting can result when fixed copper sprays are applied after bloom.

Plate 3.4
Dark, sunken spots are an obvious symptom of bitter pit.

Plate 3.5
Adult codling moths.

Plate 3.6
Codling moth eggs and larva.

Plate 3.7
When codling moths are caught in a 10-milligram pheromone trap, surrounding fruit should be examined for eggs or damage.

Plate 3.8
Shoots can be permanently damaged by rosy apple aphid.

Harvest and Postharvest Operations

Plate 4.1
Apples are stained with iodine:potassium iodide to estimate starch content. A cross-section of the apple is dipped in the solution for 30 seconds and rinsed in water to remove excess solution. Then the starch content is recorded. A score of 0=100 percent staining, and 6=0 percent staining.

Plate 4.2
For the Granny Smith variety, the California Granny Smith Apple Starch Scale is used for determining harvest maturity. A 30-apple sample must average a score of 2.5 (or greater) before harvest can begin.

Plate 4.3
Apple firmness is determined using a penetrometer fitted with a 7/16-inch (11-mm) tip. The fruit skin is first removed, and then the force required to press the probe into the flesh is measured.

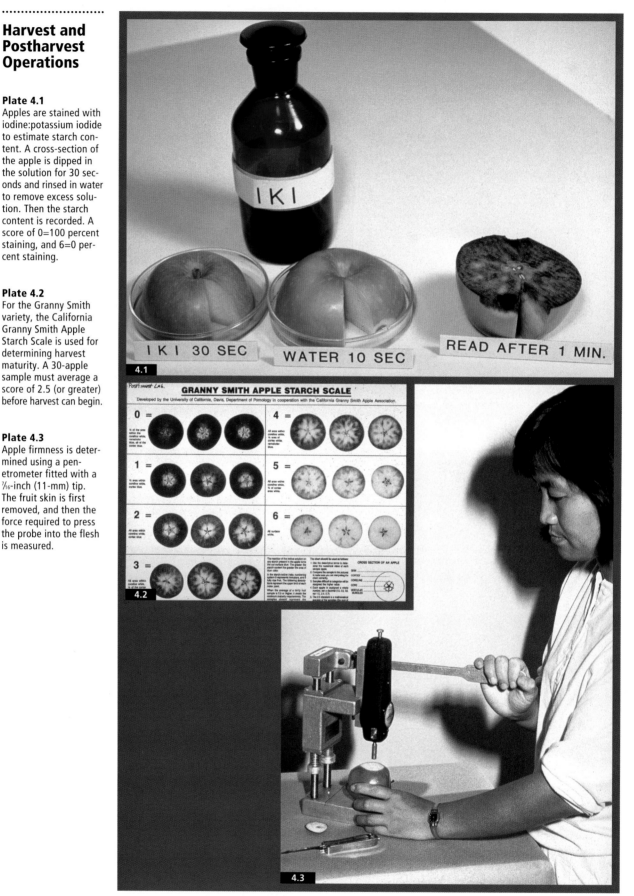

BIBLIOGRAPHY

....

WORKS CITED

Jolly, Desmond A. 1989. Consumer willingness to pay price premiums for organic apples and peaches. University of California, Davis, Dept. of Agricultural Economics. March.

— 1996. Consumer profiles of buyers and nonbuyers of organic produce. In *Organic '92: Proceedings of the organic farming symposium*. Oakland: University of California Division of Agriculture and Natural Resources Publication 3356.

Jolly, Desmond A., Howard Schutz, Jagjit Johal, and Kathy Diaz-Knauf. 1989. Marketing organic foods in California: Opportunities and constraints. University of California, Sustainable Agriculture Research and Education Program, Research Report, August.

Klonsky, Karen, Laura Tourte, Chuck Ingels, and Sean Swezey. 1994. U.C. Cooperative Extension production practices and sample costs to produce organic apples for the fresh market. Davis, CA: University of California Cooperative Extension.

Kozlowski, Perry. 1999. Personal communication to Paul Vossen. February 19.

Lobo, Ramiro W., D. Wallace, S. Parker, and D. Jolly. 1998. Farmers' markets: Consumer preferences and shopping patterns. Unpublished study. University of California Cooperative Extension, San Diego.

Thompson, Gary, and Julia Kidwell. 1998. Explaining the choice of organic produce: Cosmetic defects, prices, and consumer preference. *American Journal of Agricultural Economics*, 80:277-287.

....

UNIVERSITY OF CALIFORNIA AGRICULTURE AND NATURAL RESOURCES (ANR) PUBLICATIONS

Apple Scab Management (Publication 21412, 1985)

Commercial Apple Growing in California (Publication 2456, 1992)

Compost Production and Utilization (Publication 21514, 1995)

Covercrops for California Agriculture (Publication 21471 [English], 1989; Publication 21510 [Spanish], 1996)

Directory: Information Sources for Marketing California Fresh Fruits and Vegetables (Publication 21480, 1990)

Integrated Pest Management for Apples & Pears, 2nd ed.(Publication 3340, 1999)

Irrigating Deciduous Orchards (Publication 21212, 1981)

Managing Insects and Mites with Spray Oils (Publication 3347, 1991)

Micro-Irrigation of Trees and Vines (Publication 3378, 1996)

Natural Enemies Are Your Allies! (Poster 21496, 1991)

Organic Farming Directory (Family Farm Series, Publication 21479, 1990)

Pests of the Garden and Small Farm: A Grower's Guide to Using Less Pesticide, 2nd ed. (Publication 3332, 1999)

Propagation of Temperate Zone Fruit Plants (Publication 21103, 1979)

Pruning Fruit and Nut Trees (Publication 21171, 1980)

Regulations Governing Contracts between Growers and Handlers of Agricultural Produce: A Primer for Small-Scale Producers (Publication 21425, 1987)

Small-Scale Cold Rooms for Perishable Commodities (Publication 21449, 1996)

Soil and Plant Tissue Testing in California (Publication 1879, 1983)

Soil Solarization: A Nonpesticidal Method for Controlling Diseases, Nematodes, and Weeds (Publication 21377, 1997)

Sustainable Agriculture for California: A Guide to Information (Publication 3349, 1991)

UC IPM Pest Management Guidelines - Apples (Publication 3339, 1998)

Water Quality: Its Effects on Ornamental Plants (ANR Publication 2995, 1985)

The above publications are available from

University of California
ANR Communication Services
6701 San Pablo Avenue
Oakland, CA 94608
800-994-8849 or 510-642-2431
FAX 510-643-5470
http://anrcatalog.ucdavis.edu/

ADDITIONAL INFORMATION

"Controlling Codling Moth in Backyard Orchards" is a free leaflet available from

University of California,
Santa Cruz
Center for Agroecology &
Sustainable Food Systems
1156 High Street
Santa Cruz, CA 95064
831-459-3240
FAX: 831-459-2799
http://zzyx.ucsc.edu/casfs/

INTERNET RESOURCES

Fruit and Nut Information Center, UC Davis
http://pom44.ucdavis.edu/

Small Farm Center
http://www. sfc.ucdavis.edu/

UC Statewide Integrated Pest Management Project
http://www.ipm.ucdavis.edu/

UC Sustainable Agriculture Research and Education Program
http://www.sarep.ucdavis.edu/

INDEX